SPORT
EDUCATION

Quality PE Through Positive Sport Experiences

Daryl Siedentop, PED
The Ohio State University

Editor

W9-ATZ-528

Human Kinetics

Library of Congress Cataloging-in-Publication Data

Sport education : quality PE through positive sport experiences /
   Daryl Siedentop, editor.
      p.   cm.
   Includes bibliographical references (p.   ) and index.
   ISBN 0-87322-435-3
   1. Sports for children--Study and teaching.   I. Siedentop, Daryl.
   GV709.2.S663   1994
   796'.01922--dc20   93-42450
                                                          CIP

ISBN: 0-87322-435-3

Acquisitions Editor: Rick Frey, PhD; **Developmental Editor**: Mary E.
Fowler; **Assistant Editors**: Lisa Sotirelis, Matt Scholz, Dawn Roselund, and
Jacqueline Blakley; **Copyeditor**: Tom Plummer; **Proofreader**: Karen Dor-
man; **Production Director**: Ernie Noa; **Typesetter and Text Layout**:
Yvonne Winsor; **Text Designer**: Jody Boles; **Cover Designer**: Jody Boles;
Photographer (cover): Jack Davis; **Interior Art**: Kathy Boudreau-Fuoss
and Studio 2D; **Printer**: United Graphics

Printed in the United States of America

10   9   8   7   6   5   4   3   2   1

Human Kinetics
P.O. Box 5076, Champaign, IL 61825-5076
1-800-747-4457

Canada: Human Kinetics, Box 24040, Windsor, ON N8Y 4Y9
1-800-465-7301 (in Canada only)

Europe: Human Kinetics, P.O. Box IW14, Leeds LS16 6TR, England
0532-781708

Australia: Human Kinetics, P.O. Box 80, Kingswood 5062
South Australia
618-374-0433

New Zealand: Human Kinetics, P.O. Box 105-231, Auckland 1
(09) 309-2259

To my parents, Dorothy and Russell, who
gave so much of themselves for my sport education.

Contents

Preface

Sport is an excellent vehicle for reaching physical education objectives. *Sport Education* is a teacher-tested model that has won the support of teachers and students alike. In this book we show how sport participation can help children and youth to become skillful in game play, become aware of fair play, become knowledgeable and skillful in other areas of sport (such as managing, refereeing, and score keeping), and become better equipped to function effectively as both leaders and team players.

Everyone knows there are widespread abuses in sport, from children's sport right up through elite, professional sport. That provides the impetus for physical educators to teach sport in a way that helps all children and youth learn to value fair play, respect officials, respect opponents, and appreciate the beauty of an evenly contested, well-played game. Sport, when taught properly, provides important developmental experiences for children and youth, not only through increased playing competence but also through personal growth and responsibility.

Sport education has been particularly successful in contributing to the students' personal growth. Sport education puts students into positions of responsibility, and their success in those roles is important to team and sport season success. In sport education, students gradually assume more responsibility for their own educational experience. Students are expected to contribute to decision making within their teams and within the class. Team members, with the help of their teacher, deal with problems when they arise. Personal growth results.

You won't see 12-member volleyball teams or 14-member softball teams playing against one another in sport education. Sport education is developmentally sensitive: small-sided games are used, and rules, equipment, and playing conditions are modified to ensure full participation and success.

My colleagues and I have written this book for teachers. The curricular plans and instructional strategies we describe have been tested and retested. With this book, any teacher will be able to get started in sport education immediately. We provide examples that can be lifted and used by teachers who might want or need an easy entry into the model. The model also allows for variations that are required by local factors unique to each teaching context, and provides ample room for you to create new forms of sport education.

Presentation of this text is straightforward. We have divided it into three parts. In Part I, chapter 1 explains ideas underlying the model, and chapter 2 presents the curricular and instructional principles necessary to implement it. We use examples drawn from actual school programs so that teachers can grasp quickly how the sport education model can fit into their local school programs.

Part II contains seven chapters that show how the program has been used at the elementary, middle, and high school levels. These chapters included complete descriptions of sport education programs that have been tested in schools. Sufficient details of planning and procedures are presented such that any teacher can begin to use the model immediately. Chapters 5 and 9 show how the model can be utilized as a curriculum model at the elementary and secondary levels.

Part III shows how sport education can be evaluated and extended. It includes a chapter on authentic assessment through sport education. It also includes a chapter showing how the sport education model can be extended to an Olympic curriculum.

We have purposely chosen different kinds of sports to illustrate the model—gymnastics, volleyball, soccer, tennis, and even a fitness oriented activity such as weight training. The variations at the elementary, middle, and high school levels provide interesting contrasts, with ideas that can be adapted from one level to another. Ideas for motivating students, as well as for establishing accountability and grading schemes, are included.

The major immediate benefits of sport education are best described by the reports of teachers who have used the model. Student enthusiasm increases. Students voluntarily seek time for extra practice and instruction. Students become more responsible, and as they do teachers begin to develop relationships with them that go beyond compliance. Nonparticipant and low-skilled students become active and valued members of teams and often benefit more than in conventional instructional models.

I am convinced that sport education can increase the impact of physical education as a school subject, moving it from the marginal status it now too often occupies to a more central, valued place in the school curriculum. *Sport Education* shows how to implement a true "sport-for-all" ethic and to educate students so that they are not only more knowledgeable games players, but also are stronger advocates for good sport practices in the larger sport culture.

I am deeply indebted to all the teachers who have used the sport education model and have helped to develop it further with their energy and creativity, and I am especially indebted to the teachers who contributed to this text.

Daryl Siedentop
Columbus, Ohio

PART
I

Introduction to Sport Education

Most physical education teachers teach sport as part of the curriculum. Part I introduces methods to teach sport more fully and more authentically in physical education. Chapter 1 explains the underlying principles of sport education; chapter 2 describes how to implement the model.

Once you have read these chapters, you will understand that saying "I just completed my volleyball unit" or "I'm going to start on a tennis unit soon" means something quite different in the sport education model than in the traditional context of teaching sport in physical education. All the evidence suggests that your students will notice the differences immediately and will be enthusiastic and supportive of this new way to teach sport.

We all know that many boys and girls love sport and love to be on a team. Many physical educators have been concerned that students who are less skilled or less socially accepted by peers are typically left out of opportunity and camaraderie when sports are taught and played in physical education. Sport education solves that concern because it gives all students the chance to know and love sport and the opportunity to have a good educational and social experience as part of a team.

Many of us now believe that continuing the business-as-usual approach to physical education in schools puts us at increasing risk in the curriculum. Students, parents, and administrators expect more, and sport education provides a means to fulfill their expectations.

CHAPTER
1

The Sport Education Model

Daryl Siedentop
The Ohio State University

Sport education is a curriculum and instruction model developed for school physical education programs. That may not sound new, let alone revolutionary; indeed, sport skills and games have been taught in physical education for most of this century. Still, as I explain the model, you will find that sport education is not business as usual. You might even agree that sport education has the potential to revolutionize PE.

Sport education provides experiences that are more complete and authentic than typical PE sport. In this model students not only learn more completely how to play sports but also to coordinate and manage their sport experiences. They also learn individual responsibility and effective group membership skills.

Teachers in third grade through high school classes have developed the sport education model following its initial trials in several elementary schools in central Ohio. As teachers at different grade levels and places heard about the projects, they too became interested in trying sport education. These teacher-trials resulted in modifications that enriched and extended the model. Every example and feature of sport education described in this book has been tried in schools.

Sport education went well the first time I tried it. I enjoyed it and, more importantly, the children really enjoyed it too!

—Elementary PE specialist

The sport education model spread more rapidly after published materials appeared (Siedentop, 1987; Siedentop, Mand, & Taggart, 1986). More recently, a nationwide curriculum project in New Zealand high schools used the model (Grant, 1992).

Sport Education Goals

The sport education model has considerably more ambitious goals than most PE sport programs. It seeks to educate students to be *players* in the fullest sense and to help them develop as competent, literate, and enthusiastic sportspeople.

- A *competent* sportsperson has sufficient skills to participate in games satisfactorily, understands and can execute strategies appropriate to the complexity of play, and is a knowledgeable games player.
- A *literate* sportsperson understands and values the rules, rituals, and traditions of sports and distinguishes between good and bad sport practices, whether in children's or professional sport. A literate sportsperson is both a more able participant and a more discerning consumer, whether fan or spectator.
- An *enthusiastic* sportsperson participates and behaves in ways that preserve, protect, and enhance the sport culture, whether it is a local youth sport culture or a national sport culture. As members of sporting groups, such enthusiasts participate in further developing sport at the local, national, or international levels. The enthusiastic sportsperson is involved.

These goals are lofty. Physical educators must understand and believe that in teaching the forearm pass, the foot trap, or a zone defense they contribute not only those specific outcomes but also, in a sense, to society.

Sport Education Objectives

Sport education has immediate and comprehensive objectives, which students can achieve through their participation:

- Develop skills and fitness specific to particular sports.
- Appreciate and be able to execute strategic play in sports.
- Participate at a level appropriate to their stage of development.
- Share in the planning and administration of sport experiences.
- Provide responsible leadership.
- Work effectively within a group toward common goals.

- Appreciate the rituals and conventions that give particular sports their unique meanings.
- Develop the capacity to make reasoned decisions about sport issues.
- Develop and apply knowledge about umpiring, refereeing, and training.
- Decide voluntarily to become involved in after-school sport.

Is it possible to achieve these comprehensive objectives in regular physical education programs? Yes—but probably not with a business-as-usual approach to organizing and teaching the program.

Because of the time frame [students] developed in confidence, learned the rules, improved in skills, umpired, and helped teammates. These things seldom happen in physical education in such a positive way. Let's be honest.

—Secondary PE teacher

Long–Term Implications

What if sport education was done everywhere and done well? What would be the effects? Over a long term, sport education aims to contribute to a sound, sane, and humane sport culture that maximizes participation. The major ethic of sport education is "sport in all its forms for all the people."

Sport cultures evolve. They get better in some ways and worse in others. The widespread interest in children's and youth sport over the past several decades is evidence of how central a developmental experience sport has become. Many people share a major concern that the experience is not always educationally sound. The extraordinary interest in professional and Olympic sport testifies to the degree to which elite sport has become central to the economic and cultural life of nations. Elite sport, however, is too often tainted with problems that diminish the sport itself, and athletes are often used and abused for economic or political purposes.

A second long-term purpose of sport education is to ensure that sport involvement at all levels is designed primarily for the benefit of participants. Practices that might harm either individual participants or the sport itself should be reduced or eliminated. Achieving this purpose requires increasing numbers of literate and enthusiastic sportspeople who have the knowledge to protect and develop sport practices and the commitment to spend time and energy in such pursuits.

A third long-term purpose of sport education is to make sport more widely accessible so that gender, race, disability, socioeconomic status, and age are not barriers to participation. Sport in all its forms for all the people is a good slogan, but for it to become fully operational as a cultural ethic will require a new generation of sportspeople committed to making the slogan a reality.

Who will educate that new generation? I contend that physical educators bear this responsibility, simply because physical education provides the best opportunity to reach more children and youth because schools reach the largest percentage of children and youth, unlike extracurricular children's and youth sport programs where gender, race, disability, and socioeconomic status are still too often barriers to participation. If "sport in all its forms for all the people" is a worthy ethic, then physical educators—in their roles as sport educators—have the potential to become the grass-roots guardians of a healthy, sane, participatory sport culture.

Sport Education in Physical Education

Let me make it clear that I don't advocate that physical education should be transformed totally into sport education. Sport education is not meant to replace physical education. It is not meant to reduce or eliminate attention to physical fitness, dance, leisure pursuits, and adventure education. Although chapter 8 shows how fitness can be developed in high school within the sport education model, this does not suggest that fitness is not an important goal of physical education, nor does it suggest that other kinds of fitness programs in physical education are not worthy. Many youth and adults have strong interests in outdoor leisure activities, and although these too no doubt could be done within the sport education instructional model, that fact does not mean that they are sports per se, nor does it diminish their importance as a distinct area of PE. Chapter 9 shows how sport education can be conceptualized as a part of the total physical education program at the high school level.

Having made it clear that I see sport education as one part of the physical education program, let me also make it clear that I disagree completely with the notion that sport should not be part of the physical education curriculum at all. I have seen it heard and argued—by physical educators—that sport should not be part of the curriculum because it is too competitive, it neglects the less-skilled student, it is the responsibility of the community rather than the school, it promotes elitism, or because the heterogeneous nature of most physical education classes makes it too difficult to teach. There is no doubt that these problems occasionally occur in physical education but are they inevitable? The evidence presented in this book by teachers shows that appropriate use of the sport education model eliminates these problems.

This was a real mountain [challenge] from the start and to see it go through and generate the enthusiasm it did was quite worthwhile... particularly over things that I am often reluctant at letting the kids do .... To see the kids pick [the sport education model] up and run with it with all kids getting some benefit was unbelievable.

—Secondary PE teacher

Differences Between Sport Education and Physical Education

Sport education grew out of my dissatisfaction with seeing sport taught incompletely and inadequately in many physical education classes. Typical physical education teaches *sport skills* and *recreational games*. In a volleyball unit, for example, I've seen the serve, forearm pass, and set taught independently as isolated skills. Then the basic rules are introduced and students are organized into teams so that games can be played, often large-sided games where the demands of the game are not well matched to the developmental levels of the students. Strategy is noticeably absent. The skills, learned incompletely and in isolation, are seldom displayed appropriately in the game context. The game, for most students, isn't even much fun because their skills are inadequate and they haven't been taught to appreciate and execute the strategies involved. As a result, many students derive the fun in playing volleyball from social interaction rather than from playing a game well. Other students are simply bored because they are involved in what is clearly a trivial activity.

Sport in physical education has typically been decontextualized. This happens in several ways. Skills are taught in isolation rather than as part of the natural context of executing strategy in game-like situations. The rituals, values, and traditions of a sport that give it meaning are seldom even mentioned, let alone taught in ways that students can experience them. The affiliation with a team or group that provides the context for personal growth and responsibility in sport is noticeably absent in physical education. The ebb and flow of a sport season is seldom captured in a short-term sport instruction unit. It became clear that, too often, physical education teaches only isolated sport skills and less-than-meaningful games. Students are not educated in sport.

Sport education grew out of these observations and concerns. It grew out of the desire to make the educational sport experience for boys and girls in physical education more authentic and complete. The direction of sport education became clear when the way in which sport is taught in physical education was compared to the way sport is typically organized and implemented in youth sport, school sport, and club or organized recreational sport.

Major Characteristics of Sport Compared to Physical Education

Figure 1.1 illustrates the typical context for sport. Six primary features characterize institutionalized sport and give sport the special meaning that makes it different from other forms of motor activity. These features are often neglected or are absent when sport is taught in physical education.

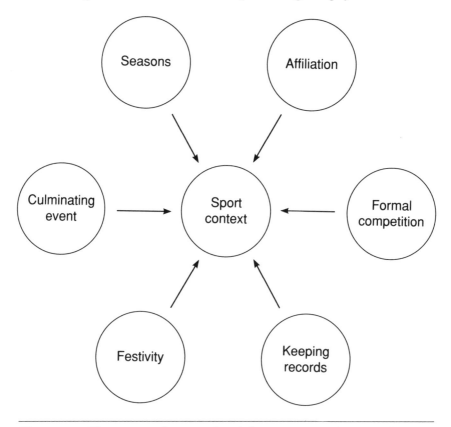

Figure 1.1 The primary features that define institutional sport and provide unique meanings for participation.

Seasons. Sport is done by seasons, and seasons are long enough to allow for significant experience. A sport season encompasses both practice and competition, and often ends with a culminating event. Physical education is organized in units that are often of short duration, sometimes lasting no longer than five to six lessons.

Affiliation. Players are members of teams or clubs and tend to retain membership throughout the season. Much of the meaning derived from sport participation and a large part of the personal growth that can result from good sport experiences is intimately related to affiliation. In physical education, students are members of the same class, but in terms of sport activity their team affiliation changes from day to day and often within the same lesson.

Formal Competition. Sport seasons are defined by formal competition that is interspersed with practice sessions and occurs in different formats: dual meets, round-robins, league schedules, and the like (see discussion of competition formats in chapter 2). The schedule is often fixed prior to the season so that teams and individuals can prepare appropriately. In physical education, there is seldom a formal competition. Because affiliation is typically absent, a formal schedule would have little meaning. The lack of affiliation and formal competition tends to make games less meaningful for participants.

Culminating Event. It is in the nature of sport to find out who is best for a particular season. The culminating competition provides goals for players to work toward. In physical education there often is a culminating event in a unit, but its meaning is diminished because of the lack of affiliation and the lack of a formal schedule leading up to the event.

Keeping Records. Records come in all forms and shapes: batting averages, shots on goal, steals, unforced errors, kills, times, distances, and the like. Records provide feedback for individuals and teams. Records help define standards and provide goals for players and teams. Records also become an important part of the traditions of a sport. In physical education, record keeping is likely to include little more than attendance, and perhaps a score on an isolated skill test.

Festivity. The festive nature of sport can be seen in the Olympic Games, Super Bowl, and World Series, where it sometimes seems to dwarf the competitions themselves. Regional track meets, the local Friday night football game, or a Little League baseball game have their own kind of festive atmosphere. The festive nature of sport enhances its meaning for participants and adds an important social element to the experience. In the typical physical education class, sport units are often devoid of any festive element.

The main features of sport—seasons, affiliation, a formal schedule of competition, a culminating event, records, and a festive atmosphere—are hardly ever reproduced in physical education classes. This is why I believe that sport has been taught incompletely and inauthentically.

Incorporating Sport Characteristics in Sport Education

The first sport education effort began quite simply by trying to incorporate the six features of sport into a physical education unit. Since then, the many teachers who have utilized the model have found ways to make the sport education experience more complete, authentic, developmentally appropriate, and educationally sound. The main characteristics of sport, when applied to sport education, require the following kinds of changes from the more traditional approaches for teaching sport in physical education.

Seasons.   Sport education seasons are longer than typical physical education units. The first sport education season was an 11-lesson unit (50 min per lesson) in an elementary school where children met once every four days, so it lasted nine weeks. A government sponsored sport education curriculum project in New Zealand high schools (Grant, 1992) produced models based on a minimum of 20 lessons. The elementary curriculum model shown in chapter 5 uses five sport seasons per school year. The high school model shown in Chapter 9 has four sport seasons per year.

We are always practicing and learning more skills. It is not like PE because in PE you are practically changing what you are doing every period.

—High school student

Sport education units are longer for two reasons. First, there is more to accomplish because sport is taught more completely and more authentically. Second, it takes more time for students to learn to be competent games players so that strategic play within competitions reaches an appropriate level, given the backgrounds and developmental capabilities of the students.

Affiliation.   In sport education, students quickly become members of teams and maintain that affiliation through the season. Team membership allows for role differentiation and individual responsibility relative to the group, which, in turn, creates the potential for self-growth. Team membership creates enthusiasm. It can also create problems, but it is in working through those problems of peer relationships within teams that children and youth grow and mature. Students typically have different team affiliations with each new season (in the elementary model in chapter 5, students are members of a team for the school year).

Formal Competition.   In sport education, a formal schedule of competition is arranged early in the season. The formal schedule often requires that teams make decisions about optimizing team performance in various competitions. The formal schedule allows for individual and group goals to be set. The sport education season focuses heavily on practice early in the season as team members learn skills and teams develop strategies. As the season progresses, less time is devoted to basic practice and more time is devoted to competition and to competition-specific practice. The elementary soccer model shown in chapter 3 describes how progressively more complex competitions can be used to gradually introduce more complex skills and strategies. The formal schedule allows for teams to prepare for upcoming competitions by working on weaknesses or preparing new strategies. The format for scheduling competition can be as diverse as the world of sport.

Culminating Event.   In sport education, the season ends with a culminating event. This might be a one-day track and field meet, a 3 vs. 3 volleyball championship, a gymnastic team competition, or the bringing together of place winners from two separate competitions. The culminating event should be festive, designed to provide a fitting climax to a sport season. It should also involve all participants, because total participation is one of the ways that sport education differs from other forms of sport.

Record Keeping.   In sport education, records are kept and used to enhance the educational experience. Records can be as simple as shots on goal and saves for a 2 vs. 2 soccer competition for fourth graders or as complex as complete sets of basketball statistics (shooting percentages, rebounds, steals, assists, and turnovers) for tenth graders. They can also involve judging performance as in gymnastics, diving, or skating, with students acting as judges. Records have many uses. They provide feedback for individual and group performance. They can be used to set goals for future competitions. Records provide teachers with an authentic form of assessment. They provide part of the local tradition of the sport within a school, such as the fifth grade girls' team long jump record, the top score in balance beam for seventh graders, or the highest team total of the year for aces in a team tennis competition.

Festivity. In sport education, teachers attempt to make each season festive. Teams have names and can develop uniforms. Records are publicized. Individual and group performance is recognized and appreciated. The gym can be decorated for a culminating event. The rituals and traditions of the sport are emphasized and honored.

These characteristics are present in nearly all sport education units, regardless of school level or sport. You will see these characteristics expressed differently in the many examples in this book, but they will all be present in each example.

How Sport Education Differs From Sport

Having described how we have tried to make sport education more similar to authentic forms of sport, I now need to emphasize several important ways in which it differs from youth sport, interschool sport, and elite sport. There are three ways in which sport education differs from institutional sport—participation requirements, developmentally appropriate involvement, and more diverse roles. These differences are due to the fact that our model is concerned with sport education, not merely sport activity.

Participation Requirements. Sport education demands full participation at all points in the season by all students. This consideration affects the size of teams and the nature of competitions, among others. Elimination tournaments are not appropriate. Large teams are not appropriate because research shows that having too many students on a side during play means that play will be dominated by more-skilled students (Siedentop, 1990). Culminating events should be events for all students, not just the top finishers or teams. All students experience all roles, not just the more gifted students or the natural leaders.

Developmentally Appropriate Involvement. The forms of sport used in sport education need to be developmentally matched to the experience and abilities of the students. My own view is that no full-sided, adult form of sport is appropriate for sport education. Teachers have had more success with soccer competitions that begin with 1 vs. 1 or 2 vs. 2 and seldom move beyond 5 vs. 5. In basketball or volleyball 3 vs. 3 is useful even for high school students. The nature of the game also has to be modified in most cases, even though it is important to preserve the essence of the game. For example, badminton is a racket sport with the objective of hitting the shuttlecock so it lands within the opposite court boundaries but cannot be returned by the opponent. This means that court sizes are smaller; nets are higher or lower than normal, depending on purpose; rules are modified; and equipment is changed to make the game more friendly for students—all without changing the basic nature of the contest.

Diverse Roles. Sport education assigns students more roles than is typical for children's, youth, or school sport, where the only role to learn is performer. In sport education students learn to be coaches, referees, and scorekeepers. In some sport education variations, they also can learn to be managers, publicists, broadcasters, and trainers. Thus, sport education contributes not only to a more complete understanding of sport but also to a form of career education for sport-related professions.

Developmentally Appropriate Competition

One of the reasons sport has been downplayed or taught only in restricted forms within physical education is that teachers fear the many abuses of competition that occur all too regularly in interschool, collegiate, and elite sport. Many of these abuses are attributed to an overemphasis on competition, a win-at-all-costs philosophy, that far too often is related to economic gains that have little to do with sport as sport, or the well-being of participants. This issue needs to be faced straightforwardly because it is a legitimate educational concern. Sport education provides the vehicle through which these abuses can be eliminated as children and youth learn about and experience educationally appropriate competition.

Sport education presents developmentally appropriate competition to all students regardless of skill level, gender, or disability. The issue in sport education is not too much or too little competition, but appropriate competition. There is much to be learned from appropriate competition, both individually and as a member of a competitive group: The biggest lesson is to play hard, play fair, honor your opponent, and accept that when the contest is over, it is over. What matters most is taking part fairly and honorably, not which individual or team wins or loses. These lessons need to be taught and reinforced as key components of sport education.

There is also a widespread, general misunderstanding of what competition means, and it is fair to suggest that in sport education students have the opportunity to learn the broader meaning of competition just as they have the opportunity to experience a more complete and authentic form of sport.

Competition has three central meanings (Siedentop, 1981):

- It is first of all a festival.
- It has a deeply important meaning related to the pursuit of competence.
- It refers to various states of rivalry.

Sadly, the latter meaning is generally assumed by most laypersons.

Festivity

A fundamental meaning of *competition* is to come together, which refers to the festive nature of the word. This meaning of competition is least understood and often neglected. Festivals mark significant events and are typically laden with ritual and tradition. Certainly, all of us have experienced a great sports festival of one kind or another. Festivals are meant to be celebrated! Thus, it is incumbent upon sport educators to find ways to help students learn to celebrate their participation in sport by creating a festive atmosphere.

Pursuit of Competence

A second meaning of competition, one that is particularly important to an ongoing involvement in sport, is the pursuit of competence. Clearly, the words *compete* and *competence* are etymologically related. A sport competition creates a forum where participants test themselves, set new goals, pursue those goals, and then test themselves again. Thus, standards of performance and records are important to sport. In the pursuit of competence, competition is almost never against someone or some team; It is a contest with oneself to surpass objective standards of performance.

Rivalry

The third, and more common, meaning of competition is rivalry. There are many different kinds of rivalries in sport: person against person, team against team, and person against a clock or other objective standard. Some would have us believe that sport is a zero-sum competition in which one person or team wins only to the extent that another person or team loses. However, discussion with athletes immediately reveals the silliness of such a proposition. Imagine telling 5,000 runners who have just completed a 42K marathon race that they are all losers because they didn't finish first! Imagine telling a team that had improved its record dramatically to finish a strong third place in an eight-team league that it is a loser because it didn't win the championship! Indeed, rivalry tends to have its strongest meaning when it is clearly viewed as part of the festive nature of competition and in terms of the standards and traditions that are created by the sport forums where competence is pursued. These are the meanings of competition that underlie sport education.

Your Role as Teacher

Sport education is not a throw-out-the-ball model where you abdicate your professional responsibilities. It is true that as students gain experience in sport education and as students become more mature they take on more of the responsibilities for the sport education season. However, it is just as true that we are still the architects of the educational environment and the persons who are ultimately responsible for its efficiency and vitality.

To create maximum time for sport education, we must be good planners and class managers. This means developing managerial and transitional routines that save time and minimize disruptions (Siedentop, 1991). Because there are many roles to learn in sport education, we must define those roles, teach them, and design good practice with feedback so students can learn their roles well. Because skill and strategy development are key concepts in nurturing knowledgeable games players, you must help students to acquire game-related skills and to understand and be able to execute a range of strategies.

I have always been concerned about the social interaction aspect of phys ed and how you change the attitudes of boys and girls and their roles in sport. I have come to the conclusion that it doesn't work [producing positive outcomes] in a 1:30 ratio with the teacher dominating. You can change attitudes when [students] are working on things subconsciously in a small team. This unit [sport education] has produced outcomes that I have been trying for years to produce in a normal situation.

—Secondary PE teacher

Because values and fair play are so central to sport education, you must above all explain, model, and provide purposeful practice for good sporting behavior, not in the abstract, nor on a written test, but when it counts, during competition itself. Values and attitudes are formed slowly and need to be attended to constantly. This requires that you design an educational environment where fair play and sporting values are taught, practiced, and reinforced consistently.

The models shown in the various chapters of this text describe variations on a theme, the theme being sport education and the variations being those designed by creative teachers to make the model work so that it reflects their values and the needs of the local context. The next chapter provides basic information necessary for you to successfully implement the sport education model in your curriculum. You now should have a good sense of what the model is about and what it is intended to accomplish. In chapter 2, we turn to the nuts and bolts of doing that well.

CHAPTER

2

Implementing the Sport Education Model

Daryl Siedentop
The Ohio State University

Like any other educational model, sport education can be done well or poorly. The success or failure of the model depends on how you implement it. This chapter has guidelines and suggestions to help you begin implementing the model and to help you subsequently to build on your success. The suggestions in this chapter come directly from teachers who have used the model.

Initial Planning

If you try sport education, then you want to be successful, for both your sake and your students. This makes planning important. Planning for a first try should take into account the particular sport, the students' level of involvement, the necessary materials to move the unit forward smoothly, and strategies for producing a festive atmosphere that motivates students. Follow these important planning suggestions.

• <u>Choose a sport you know well.</u> Sport education teachers report that heightened student interest frequently brings questions related to technique and strategy. You are effective when you can give answers to those questions quickly and confidently. Choosing a familiar sport also makes it easier to teach skills and knowledge for the roles of referee, scorekeeper, and statistician.

• Provide students opportunity for involvement. If you are accustomed to a mostly teacher-directed instructional format, it seems unwise to move to a totally student-directed format in your initial trial. You should have students occupy the main sport education roles of coach, referee, scorekeeper, and statistician, but initially they will need help in the form of clear directions and frequent feedback. You either can pick teams yourself or have students help you with the selection process. If you are at the elementary level, I'd suggest picking teams yourself for the first two or three sport seasons. You know your students' skills, cooperative abilities, and attendance records best. You can use this knowledge at the outset to ensure fair teams; as students gain experience in sport education they can gradually begin to help you choose teams. If you are at the middle or senior high school level, have students help with the selection process from the outset. Evidence strongly suggests that students will take this responsibility seriously and will try very hard to develop and maintain fair competition (Grant, 1992). As you and the students gain more experience with sport education, they can learn more roles and take more responsibility.

• Identify and prepare materials. Identify and prepare all materials you will need to make the season move forward smoothly. This refers to schedules, coaches' instructions, lineup cards, results sheets, score keeping sheets, statistics sheets, cumulative statistics records, and awards. One of the best ways teachers have found to do this is to develop a coaches' notebook that contains all the forms and is returned to the teacher after the season. A coaching notebook can have some or all of the following items:

- List of responsibilities for the coach
- Schedule of competition
- Entry forms for various competitions
- Duties of referees and scorekeepers
- Forms for assigning referees and scorekeepers for competitions
- Skill and strategy information for the sport
- Specific safety concerns coaches need to attend to
- Point system for overall team competition

Remember, the evidence suggests that students become really involved with their seasons. You don't want that motivation to be reduced by not having appropriate materials ready when they are needed.

• Make the season festive. Have students choose a team name and select a team uniform. You might have a day when they pose for a team picture of their own composition. You should also keep schedules and records up to date and in public places. The facility might get some simple, yet special decorations. Teams can be responsible for decorating bulletin boards with information and pictures related to the sport. Schedules and standings should be posted so that all students can see them. Students might create team banners or flags. The decorations and information let students know that physical education is special and important. You might also try to find ways each day to celebrate fair play, good effort, and improvement. Putting team or individual award winners' names in the school hall helps spread recognition. Having students write up their season efforts for publication in the school newspaper also is a way to share the celebration of the season.

• Plan for the "what ifs?". Finally, good planning also should take into account all of the predictable "what if?" questions related to inclement weather, loss of use of the facility due to school functions, and the like. This suggestion is not included just as business-as-usual advice to teachers, but because experience shows that students will become involved in their sport education season and will be concerned by disruptions to it.

Choosing the Sport

Sports are chosen for a variety of reasons, among which are grade level, requirements of the district course of study, equipment, facilities, and your own interests and values as a teacher. In elementary physical education, activities are typically chosen by teachers. In some secondary schools, students choose their physical education activity from among a variety of activities just as they choose other classes. The following suggestions might prove helpful.

• Younger students should experience a variety of sports over the years. This suggests that teachers make choices from invasion games (such as soccer or basketball), court-divided sports (such as volleyball or tennis), target sports (such as archery or golf), and form sports (such as gymnastics or rhythmic gymnastics). There are obviously other ways to classify sports, but the point is that somewhere during their education students should experience different kinds of sport.

• As students enter their high school years, making choices available to them improves the teaching-learning situation for both students and teachers. Even if there are just two choices per season, the fact that students are allowed to choose helps establish enthusiasm. Student choice also tends to make classes more homogeneous in skill level and background experience.

• Novel sports are often easy to teach because lack of prior experience reduces skill heterogeneity among students. Novel sports are often well accepted because of the newness. Fencing, for example, is intriguing to students and easy to teach because few students will ever have seen it, let alone ever have done it. Fencing also has specific skills and strategies and wonderfully rich rituals and traditions. If resources for equipment are scarce, you might consider a national sport from another country, such as a modified form of Australian football, team handball, or korfball, or even a relatively new sport form such as ultimate frisbee.

• As students grow more experienced in sport education, they should begin to participate in decision making about sport selection. This can be done by adding a sports council or governing board (see pages 25 and 87 for examples) to the roles in your program. Students are elected by their peers to the council, which serves to advise the teacher concerning sport education issues including sport selection.

Modifying the Sport

Sport education requires full participation. Time is always limited, and students should get as much successful experience as possible. Thus, full-sided, adult forms of sport should be avoided. Nearly all sports can be modified to make them developmentally appropriate and to ensure optimum participation by students. *Participation* means actually executing skills and being involved in strategic play as a team member. We all have seen full-sided games where some students are in the game but do not participate. Follow these suggestions for modifying specific sports.

• Use small-sided games. Research demonstrates what most teachers already know: Namely, that full-sided games are dominated by more skilled students. Low-skilled students either hide in full-sided games or are dominated. Thus, the most important way to modify a sport is to reduce the team size. We have had success teaching basic volleyball skills in a 1 vs. 1 format, using only the skills of a forearm and set passing, typically on a small court with a fairly high net (the net is raised to give students time to anticipate the direction of the ball and to get in position to return it). In a 3 vs. 3 volleyball format you can use nearly all the skill and strategy options that occur in a full-sided 6 vs. 6 format. The same reasons support using a 2 vs. 2 soccer format where students play an up-and-back strategy or in a 3 vs. 3 basketball competition where students must choose between zone and person-to-person defenses.

One good rule of thumb for elementary specialists is to keep team size equal to or less than grade level: For example, fourth graders should have teams of no more than four students. Even in the upper high school grades, the most successful participation has come with small-sided games.

• <u>Modify to create friendly playing conditions.</u> Other modifications can focus on the size of the court or field, the nature and size of equipment, and the rules. Most rules should encourage continuous play: for example, in soccer students may retrieve an out-of-bounds ball and play on by dribbling the ball in bounds themselves or passing it to a teammate. Smaller balls, softer balls, shorter equipment, nearer or lower targets, and larger goals all create a more friendly game for students and increase their chances for success without altering the basic nature of the sport.

• <u>Games should typically be of short duration.</u> This helps to focus the intensity and reduces lopsided scores. Managerially, it is helpful to have all games begin and end at the same time. For example, you might have 6 to 8 min, running-time, half-court 2 vs. 2 basketball games going on at four baskets. With one referee, one scorekeeper, and one statistician at each court, this format keeps 28 students fully occupied at all times. If you add one student coach for each team at each court, the format fully involves 36 students. At the end of 6 to 8 min all games end. During a 2 to 3 min interim, captains get the next teams ready to play at their assigned courts, referees get to their next assignments, and scorekeepers from the first game turn in performance records while scorekeepers for the next game get the appropriate forms and go to their assigned places.

At the elementary level, teachers have had success with 3 to 4 min games. The length of game that works best is partially a function of length of teaching lesson. Also, as games get more complex with larger-sided teams, game length can increase to ensure full participation with the use of periodic substitution time-outs.

Length of Season

A primary feature of sport education is that it is done in *seasons*, which are meant to last longer than typical physical education units. The key consideration in determining an appropriate length of season is how frequently students take physical education. This determination is often difficult for teachers to make because they fear that long units will cause student boredom. I can only relate that teacher experience in sport education at all levels is consistent: students are very involved in their sport season and typically don't want it to end!

I think it's better to learn one thing and learn it well, than learn a whole lot of different things and skip over all things you need to know. Before, we were learning just how to do it . . . we never got to play a game against someone else to see how good we were. It was good to see where we were placed and if we could improve . . . become better.

—High school student

Seasons must be sufficiently long to accomplish the purposes of sport education, where students learn to be competent games players, as well as to serve as referees, scorekeepers, and in other roles. Learning to move confidently and knowledgeably as a defensive or offensive player on a team is a more difficult learning task than mastering a beginning skill in an isolated setting. These multiple learning tasks take time, more time than is typically available in a short physical education unit. Available time is a function of both length of lesson and number of lessons in a unit. This makes it difficult to establish a formula for an appropriate amount of time. However, the elementary models that have been successful have typically used 8 to 12 lessons of 45-min length or 10 to 14 lessons of 30-min length, with classes meeting once every four days or twice weekly. Secondary school models have used a minimum of 18 to 20 lessons, each lasting at least 45 min.

I haven't got time to teach the rules and skills in three weeks [six lessons] like we normally teach. To teach like that is a joke quite frankly.

—Secondary PE teacher

Selection of Teams

Sport education requires that students become members of teams early in the season and maintain their affiliations throughout. Affiliation is a key factor in promoting positive personal growth among students. Team selection will eventually be critical to the success of your program. Few issues will engender more student concern than the method of team selection.

Two major issues relate to team selection. One is team size and the other is the selection method. Team size is related to how you have modified the chosen sport and the kinds of seasonal competitions you want. For example, in elementary soccer, teachers have had great success dividing classes into three teams of 8 to 10 students each. Soccer competitions can then range between 1 vs. 1 to 6 vs. 6. A team of eight students can select several two-person teams for a 2 vs. 2 competition, yet still be able to field a six-person team. If there is only one competition, perhaps a doubles tennis competition, then teachers must decide whether they want that competition based solely on individual doubles teams or whether they want to form larger teams from which several doubles teams can be selected. The larger teams, with embedded smaller teams, is the easiest method to cover for absences and still move the season forwardly smoothly.

Five methods have been commonly used for team selection.

- Teachers can select teams ahead of time from their knowledge of students' skills, attitudes, and attendance records.
- Teachers can select (or students can elect) a sports council which, along with the teacher, makes team selections.
- Teachers can select, or students can volunteer for, the team captain, after which the teacher, along with the captains, choose fair teams. Captains are then assigned to teams by lottery.
- Students can select a sports committee that selects teams based on some performance measure or previous knowledge of peers.
- A skills test, trials, or competition ladder can be used to rank players, with the rankings in turn used for team selection.

Because one purpose of sport education is to encourage students to gradually assume more of the responsibility for directing and managing their own sport experiences, many teachers might want to begin with teacher selection, then move toward some form of student selection or joint teacher-student selection.

The following suggestions about team size and team selection have been compiled from teacher feedback and comments based on their experiences using sport education. Remember, no matter what decisions you make in these areas, students will have concerns. Team selection interests them greatly, providing a great opportunity to teach and reinforce the concept of fairness.

- Embed small teams within larger teams.   If you want more than one type of competition (singles, doubles, mixed doubles, or 2 vs. 2 and 4 vs. 4), then teams need to be large enough to accommodate the formation of different small teams from the larger team. This format enables you to have several different competitions as well as an overall, seasonal team competition. It also allows you to accommodate daily absences.

- Factor predicted absences into the selection scheme.   If you plan just a single competition (3 vs. 3 basketball) then team size and selection need to be determined primarily both by skill levels and by estimates of absences among students. However, even with a single competition format, there is much to be gained by having larger teams from which smaller teams are selected. This covers the absence problem. It also allows for graded competition, that is, an *A* competition and a *B* competition. It would also allow for a boys' competition, girls' competition, and mixed competition, all selected from the larger mixed team.

• Use uneven numbers of teams to create a duty team. Many teachers have had success using a duty team for their competitions. A duty team, rather than playing, fills the roles of referee, scorekeeper, and statistician. For example, if you have three teams for a competition, then one team can rotate into the duty team role for each series of contests. This format suggests using an uneven number of teams.

• Establish clear criteria for appointment of student-selectors. When students are elected by classmates to select teams, establish clear criteria for their election. When classes elect selectors, sport council members, or the like, it is important to establish that good judgment is the key criterion for the positions, and that all students should be considered, not just top performers.

• Establish clear criteria for team selection. When students help with selection, it is essential that they understand the criteria to be used. Selection panels should consider skill and fitness levels, balancing gender and race among teams, evenly dispersing students with leadership potential, balancing frequently absent students among teams, and avoiding placing on the same teams students who are known to have conflicts. Discussions concerning selection should remain confidential within the selection panel. Again, this process provides an excellent opportunity to teach and reinforce concepts of fairness and responsibility.

• Consider time-resource trade-offs for objective selection. If a skill test, trials, or competition ladder is used, selection should be accomplished quickly. Teachers should consider the trade-offs involved in a more objective selection process and the time used to establish performances. Although the selection process needs to be fair, it should not take away substantial time from the actual sport education season.

• Selection should take place when students are reasonably familiar with the sport they will learn. This suggests that selection in unfamiliar sport units should take place a bit later than for sport units where students have previous experience with the activity.

Student Roles Within the Team

The main roles that define the basic sport education model are coach or captain, referee, scorekeeper, and statistician. Other roles that teachers have used successfully in sport education are publicist, manager, trainer, sports council member, and broadcaster. Each of these roles needs to be defined clearly. Whatever roles are utilized should be included in the accountability system. You can't expect students to apply themselves to a role unless it counts for the team and their individual assessment.

Although the specific nature of roles differs from situation to situation, the following are common assignments.

- *Coaches* or *captains* lead warm-ups, direct skill and strategy practice, help make decisions about lineups, turn in lineups to teachers or managers, and generally provide leadership for their teams.

- *Assistant coaches* or *captains* help captains and take over their duties in their absence.

- *Referees* manage contests, make rule decisions, and generally keep the contest moving without undue interference.

- *Scorekeepers* record scoring performance as it occurs, keep a running account of the status of ongoing competition, compile scores, and turn over the final records to the appropriate person (teacher, manager, or statistician).

- *Statisticians* record other pertinent performance data, compile it when complete, summarize it across competitions, and turn the summarized data over to the appropriate person (teacher, publicist, or manager).

- *Publicists* take compiled records and statistics and publicize them. This has been done through weekly sport sheets, the school newspaper, posters, or a specially created sport education newsletter. The publicist occupies a role similar to what are now called sport information directors.

- *Managers* are used often to differentiate the leadership role of the coach from the administrative duties of the team. Managers turn in appropriate forms, help get team members to the right locations for their role as performers, referees, scorekeepers, and the like, and generally assume the administrative functions of ongoing team responsibilities.

- *Trainers* are responsible for knowing common injuries associated with a sport, for having access to first-aid materials, and for notifying the teacher of any injury problem during practice or competition. Although they should not administer first aid without the sanction of a teacher, they can aid the teacher in administration of first aid and in subsequent rehabilitation.

- *Sports council* (*sports board*) *members* advise teachers on issues related to the overall policies governing the sport education season and can make final decisions concerning violations of fair play rules, competition schedules, and the like.

- *Broadcasters* can introduce players and describe play during competition.

Roles are learned most easily when there are clear descriptions and expectations for role performance. One way to accomplish this is by developing a small booklet that explains the duties of each role and describes precisely the tasks that need to be accomplished and when they need to be done. This kind of booklet should be handed out to students and returned in good shape at the end of the season (teachers have had success making the return of the booklet a part of the accountability system). In the elementary model described in Chapter 5, each student has a booklet that is returned after the season. High school students typically need less direction and can be expected to act more independently as long as an accountability system keeps them on track.

Team Identity

Many students develop strong affiliations with their teams, and this should be promoted. Teams should have names and can choose a uniform, but this should be done within set criteria that take into account cost and local standards. Team photos can be done inexpensively and placed on bulletin boards or with competition schedules.

Teams should have a home practice area in the gymnasium or playing field. Team members report to this area at the start of class and do warm-ups and their own team skill and strategy practice. Home team areas also provide teachers with a convenient time saving routine for organizing students. Attendance can be taken in home areas by captains and reported to the teacher.

Teams can be encouraged to practice in nonattached time. Elementary teachers have used recess times as well as before and after school times for team practices. At higher grade levels, teams can be encouraged to practice on their own during nonattached time. Ways of including out-of-class practice in assessment and accountability systems are described throughout the text. Teams can also be encouraged to enter school intramural competitions or local, recreational competitions.

Kinds of Competition and Schedules

Sport education uses a formal schedule of competition, fixed in advance of the season so that students can prepare for it, and continue to adjust and prepare as the season progresses. Teachers can choose from among many competition formats and combinations of formats, but elimination formats should be avoided so that students continue to participate regardless of competition outcome. Remember, full participation by all students is one of the guiding ethics of sport education. Some formats follow:

- A league round-robin format such as commonly used in team sports
- Two leagues with play-offs following the regular schedule
- Multiple competitions within an overall league format, such as one would find in a tennis league where each team competition consists of girls' singles, boys' singles, and mixed doubles
- Successive round-robin competitions using the same teams, such as one might find in a soccer season that begins with 1 vs. 1, followed by 2 vs. 2, and culminates with a 4 vs. 4 competition
- Successive competitions using the same teams having different focuses, such as a gymnastics season that begins with a compulsory competition, followed by an optional competition, and culminating with an acrosport competition
- A team competition in which individuals perform in different events, such as a track and field round-robin of dual meets between teams in which team members specialize in one running event and one field event
- Competitions in which scoring is done by accumulating points based on performance standards rather than direct competition against an opponent, such as in archery, swimming, and track and field

Figure 2.1 shows a seeded tournament competition format in which all teams play the same number of contests and teams can eventually be ranked from top to bottom.

Culminating Events

Culminating events mark the end of seasons. They serve as festivals, celebrating the sport. They serve to determine champions and final placements. Culminating events add a special dimension to the sport season, but they should also serve the educational purposes of the model. Teachers must ensure that the festival aspects of the culminating event are emphasized as much or more than the rivalry aspects of the competition. The culminating event is for all the students and they all should experience it positively.

There are endless ways to define culminating events. They can have a strictly within-class focus or they can extend beyond a single class. For example, a between-classes competition can be held that pits first, second, third, fourth, and fifth place teams in the regular schedule against the same finishers from another class. Or, special balance beam, floor exercise, and bar competitions might be arranged between classes for all students who performed in those specialities.

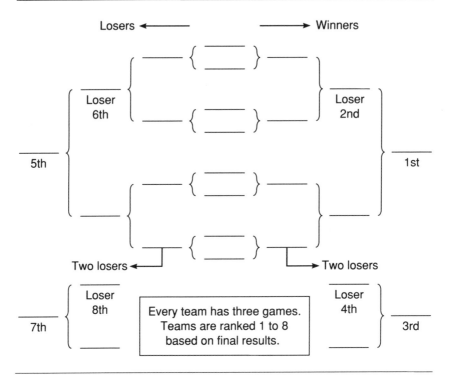

Figure 2.1 Sample format for nonelimination, seeded tournament competition.

Culminating events should be ceremonious, emphasizing the traditions and rituals of the sport. Music can accompany the entrance of teams. Team banners can identify home spaces in a gym or on a field. Players and officials can take an oath, as they do when the Olympic games begin. Players can be introduced. Special guests might be invited. If the school has a videotape machine, the event might be recorded and viewed by students at a later time. End-of-season awards should be presented.

Keeping and Using Records

A major feature of sport education is that students keep performance records that are used in various ways. One use is to provide performance feedback to individuals and groups. A second use is to publicize and celebrate improvement and accomplishment, both group and individual. A third use is to establish local standards that define the school traditions of the sport. A fourth use is to aid teachers in assessment and evaluation.

When students occupy the role of record keeper (or statistician as I have called it elsewhere) they must learn to focus on performance and accurately discriminate performance relative to the records that need to be kept. In basketball, for example, record keepers learn how to judge assists, rebounds, and steals as well as shots attempted and made. In gymnastics or aerobics competitions, middle and high school students can learn how to judge performance using a numerical rating system. This is an important way for students to learn about the sport.

As with all other roles, young or novice students should start simply; they should gradually become more sophisticated in the kind and number of records they keep. Fourth graders in floor hockey can be expected to keep shots on goal, scores, and steals. Middle school students can count blocks, kills, and service aces in volleyball. By the time students reach high school, or have several years of experience in sport education, they will be capable of complete and sophisticated record keeping.

This feature of sport education requires that teachers create easy-to-use forms for students to use during competitions. Teachers also need to ensure that students are reliable in their record keeping. Since this is a primary feature of sport education, some measure of student performance in record keeping should be part of the overall accountability system. One method is to have two students independently record the same performance data. The two records can be compared to ensure reliability of recording. Figure 2.2 shows a competition results sheet for volleyball and a way of using points for and points against as another form of competition, rather than just wins and losses.

Teaching Fair Play and Equal Competition

A primary goal of sport education is to develop good sportspersons. If that goal is to be achieved, students must learn to value fair play and equal competition. Many of the problems that plague organized sport, from youth sport through to elite, are the result of behavior by people in positions of responsibility within sport who compromise those values.

Sport education argues that good sportspersons must be more than skilled, knowledgeable games players. They must value fair play and equal competition to the extent that they are willing to behave in ways that protect those values. Eventually, students understand that sport is best for all participants when the competitions are most equal, and they understand that winning means little unless it is accomplished within the fair play conventions that govern the traditions of the sport.

Volleyball Competition Results Sheet

	Elfs	Harts	Nobs	Pumps	Dogs	Herbs
Elfs						
Harts						
Nobs						
Pumps						
Dogs						
Herbs						

Points for

	1	2	3	4	5	Total
Elfs						
Harts						
Nobs						
Pumps						
Dogs						
Herbs						

Points against

	1	2	3	4	5	Total
Elfs						
Harts						
Nobs						
Pumps						
Dogs						
Herbs						

Figure 2.2   Sample volleyball results sheet.

We sort of learned to respect each other a lot more . . . not so much harassment from everybody else . . . we were putting everybody's ideas together and working out what to do.
—High school student

The values of fair play and equal competition need to be taught as specifically and vigorously as are set passes and zone defenses.

Directions, practice, and feedback need to be devoted to these values just as they are to skills and strategies. The following suggestions will prove helpful in achieving these important educational goals.

- Ensure that the specific behaviors related to fair play are made clear to students. Elementary teachers have had success using fair play-unfair play posters that describe specific behaviors related to fair and unfair play (see page 128 for more information). Definitions of fair and unfair play tend to change by sport, so much of this teaching needs to be sport-specific. High school teachers have had success using a sports council where student members deliberate on instances of unfair play that were recorded by referees during contests or submitted to them by coaches.

- Use an accountability system that promotes and rewards fair play. Teachers have used individual and team awards for fair play. Penalties for violations of fair play rules need to be substantial. Referees should be taught how to deal with unfair play and what consequences to apply (again, these differ by sport).

- Positive, supportive spectator behavior needs to be taught and encouraged. Students should learn to support their teammates appropriately and respect the effort of their opponents.

- Use a well-defined team selection system with equal competition as a primary objective. This helps to teach and enforce the value of equal competition.

- Develop an elected sports council. The council can discuss and help to decide on issues of competition and fair play. This teaches responsibility and helps students to confront and deal with these important issues.

- Make fair play awards as important as awards for winning competitions. This has implications for how teachers arrange point systems that lead to awards.

- Teach and reward the use of rituals appropriate to the sport. Saluting the opponent in fencing, saluting judges after gymnastics competitions, and lining up teams for handshakes after a competition are ritualistic ways of showing that fair play is valued in the sport and that opponents are honored for their efforts. The real teaching goal is to have ritualistic behavior truly represent the underlying fair play ethic.

Practice Within Sport Education

Sport education is not an excuse to throw out the ball. It is not meant to be merely a series of games, nor an excuse for supervised recreation.

There are many roles to be learned, and each requires practice. Teachers typically have well-developed methods for teaching sport skills and strategies. They often have had less experience teaching students such skills as how to coach, referee, score, and keep statistics.

> *You get used to being in charge. . . . The hardest bit was stepping back. I remember the first practice they had in their teams. I gave them volleyballs, sat against the wall, and all hell broke loose. There were volleyballs going in all directions. . . . I waited and all of a sudden it just happened . . . there were coaches [students] working, there were people [team members] being trained, and it [sport education] just never looked back from there.*
>
> —Secondary PE teacher

Sport education proceeds much like a sport season. Early season sessions are devoted mainly to practicing fundamental skills and strategies. This phase involves a great deal of teaching, in some respects much as with traditional models. Captains can help. Teams can practice together in their home space. As the competition nears, practices become more specific to strategies. Mid season sees a balance of practice and competition, with practices even more specific to upcoming competitions. End-of-season sessions are dominated by competitions with just enough practice to prepare appropriately. There are also creative ways to use progressively complex competitions to introduce and practice skills and strategies. The soccer model shown in chapter 3 starts with a 1 vs. 1 competition, then moves to 2 vs. 2, 3 vs. 3, and, finally, 5 vs. 5. At each point, new skills and strategies that are appropriate to the competition are introduced. The following suggestions relate to designing good practice sessions.

• Parts of early season sessions should be devoted to learning nonperformer roles. Students should learn what violations referees look for, how they make calls, and how to keep contests moving smoothly while not unduly interfering. Students should learn how to watch contests as scorekeepers and statisticians, what performance data to collect, and how to collect and summarize it. If judging is involved, students should be taught and should discuss form and style in the sport.

• Practice sessions are taken more seriously and are more efficient if specific goals are established. In early season, much practice can be teacher directed, in many ways similar to the methods effective physical educators use in more conventional formats. As the season progresses, practices should become more specific to individual and team strengths and weaknesses. Here teachers play an important role. During competitions they should view individual and team performances and make notes. These notes can be translated into practice goals, which are discussed with or directed to team coaches, who in turn use them to determine the focus for the next team practice. The skill checklists (see page 52) and skill hustle formats (see page 74) are examples of goal-directed skill practice.

• Nonattached time can be used for team practice. Teachers have had success encouraging and rewarding such effort by including non-attached time practices as part of an overall point system. Again, however, these practices should have specific goals and a reporting mechanism so that teachers do as much as possible to make them more than mere unorganized play.

Accountability Systems

Most sport education programs have worked well because teachers have developed clear accountability systems for student performance. Examples of these systems are spread throughout the text. Chapter 10 focuses more completely on assessment.

The most common form of accountability has been the overall point system leading to end-of-season champions and awards. Teachers include in this point system all the factors for which they hold students responsible. Teams win points not only by winning contests, but also by passing tests, doing extra practices, doing warm-ups appropriately, playing fairly, turning in booklets, completing publicity assignments, and the like. From this overall point system, a host of individual and team awards can be made. The point system also determines the overall champion for the season.

Chapters 1 and 2 have provided the rationale for sport education and the means for beginning its implementation in your program. Parts II and III show you sport-specific applications at various grade levels. These examples give details about how specific sports, such as volleyball, soccer, gymnastics, and tennis, can be done in the sport education framework, and they also will show how the model is changed to apply to various grade levels.

PART
II

Curricular Examples of Sport Education

Part II presents a series of sport education applications. These were chosen to show a variety of sports done at different grade levels. Elementary applications include soccer (chapter 3) and gymnastics (chapter 4). There is also an overview of how to implement sport education as the main component in an elementary physical education curriculum (chapter 5).

The secondary applications include volleyball (chapter 6), touch rugby and tennis (chapter 7), and several fitness applications (chapter 8). Part II concludes with chapter 9, an overview of how sport education can be conceptualized as part of a comprehensive secondary physical education curriculum.

As you read each application you should think about how other sports might be done using the sport education model and how an application described for one level, for example soccer at the elementary level, might be done differently at the secondary level. To do this you will need to separate the specifics of how the sport is modified and organized for a particular grade level from how the sport education model is implemented at different developmental levels. For example, when you read the soccer chapter, you need to think about how soccer would be done differently for eighth graders and fourth graders, but you also need to think about how the suggestions for implementation in the secondary applications could be used for soccer. The following lists help to show the different ways you need to look at these chapters to end up with a thorough understanding of how you might want to develop sport education in your situation.

Sport modification	Implementation issues
What size teams would be best?	How will teams be formed?
What rules should be modified?	How will captains be chosen?
What competition format should we use?	What will I include in a point award system?
What performance data should I keep?	How will I emphasize and reward fair play?

What you will end up with is a mix-and-match understanding of how you might do badminton at the secondary level or touch football at the elementary level. You will have acquired a sufficient understanding of sport education applications so that you will know how to start your own program.

CHAPTER

3

Elementary Soccer

Chris Bell
Riverside Elementary

Jane Darnell
Olde Sawmill Elementary

This chapter describes sport education soccer for the elementary level. Its suggestions are appropriate for Grades 3-6, but could be adapted for more advanced grade levels. Adaptations would focus on more complex game combinations, assuming that students had previous soccer experience, and would allow students more responsibilities in the decision making and implementation of the soccer season.

Sport and level: soccer, Grades 3-6

Seasonal format: 10 to 12 forty-min lessons

Team membership format: teacher-selected teams; teams select captains with teacher approval

Competition format: singles, doubles, triples, and mini-soccer tournaments.

Student roles: performer, captain, referee, scorer, timer, coach

Performance records: written test, skill checkoff sheets, performance evaluation by teacher of playing and refereeing

Special features: extra practice time, intraclass meets, student notebooks, lunchtime intramurals (including cheerleaders, spectators, commentators)

Selection of Teams and Captains

Teachers should select teams that form cooperative units and are as equally skill matched as possible. This should be done based on prior knowledge of student soccer skills, their experience with the game, and their cooperation and leadership abilities. If you do not know the children's soccer skills, then a timed soccer dribbling test around obstacles can gain the necessary information. Depending on class size, two or three teams should be selected. With smaller classes, two-team formats work best. With larger classes, three-team formats are the better choice. All small-sided soccer teams will come from within the two or three large teams. For example, in a 2 vs. 2 competition, each of the two or three larger teams would enter as many two-player teams as possible. Each victory for a two-player team would count toward the larger team's total; thus, the overall competition is decided among larger teams.

Students on each team select their two captains per team. Selection can be done by secret ballot. A captain's contract is shown in Figure 3.1.

Class Procedures and Instruction

The season begins with an introduction of soccer and its history. Safety rules are stressed immediately, general procedures for the season are described, and warm-up and attendance routines are established on the first day of the season. After warming up and stretching, captains quickly distribute balls to team members to begin an independent dribbling and juggling skill warm-up. Each successive lesson will begin with the general warm-up followed by a skill warm-up; captains lead both throughout the season. The specifics of the general and skill warm-ups can be described on posters. All teams start and stop the warm-up periods together on signals from the teacher or from a tape recorder, which can also play appropriate music. In this case, the end of music would signal the end of the warm-up period. As the season progresses, the skill warm-up phase of the lesson can become more sophisticated.

The soccer skills and rules taught depend on the time allotted for the season. To begin the season, basic skills of dribbling, shielding, tackling, and shooting are introduced and practiced in preparation for a 1 vs. 1 game that will be the initial competition of the season. Refereeing and score keeping is introduced in preparation for competition.

As the season progresses, the skill and strategy instruction and practice is geared toward the progressively more complex competitions, that is, 2 vs. 2, 3 vs. 3, and 5 vs. 5. The 2 vs. 2 competition allows the teacher to introduce forward and defender positions and the skill of passing. The 3 vs. 3 competition allows for the introduction of goalie skills along with triangle passing and floor positioning. If the length

Team Captain's Contract

The captain's responsibilities are:

Demonstrate fair play
Lead team warm-ups
Report improper dress
Remind players of game times
Assign playing positions
Organize team on the field
Have good knowledge of rules
Demonstrate good safety practices
Demonstrate good class conduct

_____

Captain's signature

Team signatures:

Figure 3.1 The captain's contract sets the responsibilities for the role.

of the season permits, the season can conclude with a minigame competition with four or five players per team. This allows for even further differentiation of roles such as forwards, defenders, and goalies.

Soccer can be done quite successfully in an elementary school gymnasium. When weather or the conditions of outside fields prohibit outside play, classes can be held inside the gym. When this is done it helps to use foam balls or to slightly deflate soccer balls to allow for greater control. Cones or hot spots can delineate soccer pitches and goals. Tape or mats on walls can also be used to identify goal areas. When playing indoor soccer, it is necessary to develop an interference routine that describes what will happen when a ball from one area goes into the spaces occupied by other teams or players.

One advantage of indoor soccer is that less time is spent chasing balls. With a well established interference routine (for example, a student routine where only designated players may invade the space of another game to retrieve a ball and then only in specific ways), it might be argued that indoor soccer is more controllable than the outdoor game.

Student Roles

In this elementary model, captain is the main ongoing student role. Captains report attendance and appropriate dress at the start of each class. They lead warm-ups, manage equipment, turn in lineups, organize their players on their assigned fields or pitches, and organize their teams for noon recess practice or matches.

Each student also learns to referee soccer games and keep score and statistics during play. At the outset, simple statistics such as shots on goal and goals scored can be kept. As children gain experience, more statistics can be kept, such as steals, saves, and assists. Students can also keep time for games, giving start and stop signals.

Competitions

Soccer season encompasses a number of competitions, each designed to allow for the progressive introduction of increasingly complex skills and strategies.

One-Versus-One

The season begins with a 1 vs. 1 competition. Players are ranked for skill level: A competition for advanced players and B competition for beginners and less-experienced students. The 1 vs. 1 game is played much like half-court basketball (see Figure 3.2). After a goal is scored or when the ball is turned over, the ball is taken quickly to the back line where the player dribbles it into play to restart the game.

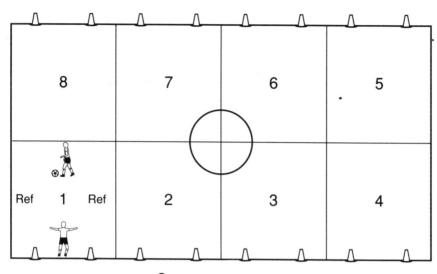

One-versus-one game
△ Cones to mark goals

Figure 3.2 Gymnasium and field organization for one-versus-one, half-court soccer competition.

If played inside, this half-court 1 vs. 1 game can be played on one eighth the floor space of a gymnasium, slowing down competition and disallowing breakaway goals so that children practice dribbling, shielding, and tackling skills with each new restart. Each pitch would have two players with a referee and scorekeeper. Captains pair team members and assign them to each competition area. Three-min games are used.

The actual competition is preceded by a scrimmage session so students can practice skills and strategies and can become familiar with the organizational setup for competition. Students not playing do the dual job of referee and coach at their assigned field or pitch. With each new 3-min game, referees rotate into play.

The format is dual round-robin tournaments, one for *A* players and one for *B* players. Each victory wins points for the overall team point total. This 1 vs. 1 game is an effective way to practice the beginning skills of dribbling, shielding, tackling, and shooting.

Two-Versus-Two

The next competition is 2 vs. 2, which can be played on a space that combines two of the 1 vs. 1 pitches shown in Figure 3.2. The actual sizes and number of pitches to establish depends on the number of children per class. Doubles teams are composed of beginners and advanced players, with a more advanced player serving as on-site coach. The forward-and-defender and up-and-back strategies are taught, along with passing and cutting skills. Each pitch would have four players, two referees, and two scorekeepers. The 2 vs. 2 competition also follows a round-robin format, with short games so that students who are refereeing and keeping score rotate into game play with each new game period. The 2 vs. 2 game consists of two periods, 3 min in length, with teammates switching positions at the half. If goalie skills have been introduced, the 2 vs. 2 game can be played as a goalie-forward combination. All games are refereed and scorekeepers can begin to keep simple performance statistics, such as shots on goal and scores. A scoresheet for a 2 vs. 2 tournament with two overall teams is shown in Figure 3.3.

Three-Versus-Three

The next competition is 3 vs. 3. Various position combinations can be used, such as two forwards and a defender; one goalie, one defender, and one forward; or two forwards and a defender-goalie. This is a good game to introduce throw-ins, goal kicks, and corner kicks. The same scrimmage and tournament format is followed and all games are refereed and scored. For inside play, the gym can be divided width-wise into three pitches. Each pitch would accommodate six players, two referees, and two scorekeepers. All games start and stop at the same time.

Minisoccer Tournament

The season culminates with a minisoccer tournament with teams of four to five players. These games are longer, with substitution time-outs at specific periods. When played inside, minisoccer games use the entire gym with pitches running lengthwise. Captains are responsible for ensuring that all players have equal playing time. This game helps students begin to understand the importance of player combinations and of always keeping a balanced team in the game. With three teams in the overall competition, it is appropriate to use one team for a duty team to provide scorers and referees. The duty team then competes in the next game and one of the other teams rotates to the duty role. A score sheet for a minisoccer tournament game is shown in Figure 3.4.

Doubles Tournament Score Sheet

Red   *Green*

Team _____   *Team* _____

Team #1 _____   Team #4 _____

Team #2 _____   Team #5 _____

Team #3 _____   Team #6 _____

Team # listed first starts with the ball. At end of game X out loser, circle the winner. With a tie, circle both.

Court _____   Court _____

Game 1	1 Plays 4 3 Refs Winner: red or green	2 Plays 5 6 Refs Winner: red or green
Game 2	4 Plays 2 1 Refs Winner: red or green	3 Plays 6 5 Refs Winner: red or green
Game 3	5 Plays 3 2 Refs Winner: red or green	6 Plays 1 4 Refs Winner: red or green
Game 4	1 Plays 5 3 Refs Winner: red or green	2 Plays 6 4 Refs Winner: red or green
Game 5	6 Plays 2 1 Refs Winner: red or green	4 Plays 3 5 Refs Winner: red or green

Poor sport conduct: Name _____   Game _____
What happened:

Figure 3.3 The score sheet for a doubles soccer tournament with two-person teams drawn from larger class teams.

Team Points and Awards

The overall competition for the soccer season is determined by teams accumulating points for a number of different activities. Teams are awarded points for class behavior, participation outside class, victories in competition, displaying fair play and cooperation, performance on written tests, and the like. Each team starts the season with 25 fair play points. Each instance of unfair play, particularly being red carded

Date _____

Grade _____

Field _____

Referee Assignments

Sideline referee	Head official

Goal line referee   Goal line referee

Sideline referee	Head scorer

Team _____   Team _____

Captain   Captain

Colors   Colors

Score: Score:

Referee (circles) the winning team

Violations—write name of any player who was carded for arguing, safety, or unfair play.

1.	1.
2.	2.
3.	3.
4.	4.

Figure 3.4 A score sheet for a minisoccer tournament of four- to five-player teams drawn from larger class teams.

during a competition, results in the loss of five points. Specifically, teams can earn points when

- all team members wear proper attire and team colors,
- captains report attendance and attire and lead warm-ups appropriately,
- all team members do stretching and skill warm-ups appropriately,
- all team members are on task throughout the lesson,
- team members encourage teammates appropriately,
- teams display fair play and cooperation,
- all team members achieve criterion on written test,
- all team members practice together at recess,
- the team plays or referees a game (one point),
- the team wins a game (one point), and
- they retain their fair play points (up to 25 points).

You should assign points for each item based on how important you think it is. For example, if you think demonstrating knowledge through written tests is important, then that should receive more points. If you have difficulty maintaining on-task behavior, then provide more points for that item and students will try harder. End-of-season awards can be given for a number of successful team performances. We typically emphasize three awards.

- The teamwork (all sport) award is given to the team that accumulates the most points throughout the season.

- Captain's awards are given to all captains who fulfill the duties and responsibilities listed in the captain's contract.

- The fair play award is given to one player in the class voted by the entire class, voted by captains, or selected by the teacher for consistently demonstrating the qualities and characteristics of fair play.

Notice that the main team award for the season is only partially determined by competitive success. The point system is geared toward recognizing and reinforcing teamwork, participation, extra practice, on-task behavior, and fair play.

Incorporating Other Soccer Activities

Soccer is an invasion game in which points are scored by putting the ball into a goal. The strategies for soccer are very much like those for lacrosse and various forms of hockey. Thus, it is easy to build on soccer experience to teach lacrosse and floor hockey or a form of field hockey. It would be an appropriate progression to teach soccer in the fourth grade, a form of field hockey in the fifth grade, and floor hockey or lacrosse in the sixth grade. In each sport, the ball is advanced through dribbling; tackling and shielding are important; and offensive strategies focus on centering to produce good shots on goal.

The instructional and competition formats described in this chapter could be used for any of these sports. When children learn a particular format, they can more easily generalize their experiences from one sport to another. When sticks are used, as in hockey and lacrosse, it is important that safety rules be introduced immediately and that substantial penalties be applied to high sticking and other unsafe behaviors.

CHAPTER
4

Elementary Gymnastics

Chris Bell
Riverside Elementary

In this chapter I describe gymnastics done as sport education in the elementary school. The suggestions are specifically appropriate to Grades 4 through 6 but can be adapted to more advanced grade levels by changing the nature and difficulty of the skills and allowing students more responsibilities in implementing the gymnastics season. You might also incorporate judging as a student role by teaching older students how to judge performances.

Sport and level: gymnastics, Grades 4-6

Seasonal format: 10 to 12 fifty-min lessons

Team membership format: captains selected by teacher; teams selected by captains with teacher approval

Competition format: compulsory meet followed by optional meet

Student roles: performer, spotter, judge, captain, spectator

Performance records: judged performances, skill checkoff sheets, written test, pretest of skills

Special features: videos of compulsory routines, video of safety rules, videotaping of performances, postseason meets between classes, extra noon practice, student notebooks

Selection of Teams and Captains

The selection of gymnastics captains is crucial to team success. You should choose captains who are responsible, cooperate well with other students, and are among the more highly skilled gymnasts. One way to select captains is to have students apply for the position, submitting a short list of qualifications or experience. Two captains should be chosen for each team. Duties can be divided equally, or one can be captain with the other as assistant.

Once you select captains, meet with them to create teams. The goal is to select teams that are well matched with respect to skill levels, boy:girl ratios, and potential problem students. One good strategy is to let captains divide the class into three teams (for a class of 20-30 students). You review the team lists to ensure fairness, then either assign captains to teams or place them by some lottery mechanism. Captains will be careful to match teams evenly because they do not know which team will be theirs. If you and the captains do not know the skill levels of the class, you can give a quick pretest to guide the selection process.

When captains and teams are selected, the first responsibilities are for each captain to return the participation contract signed by captains and team members (see Figure 4.1) and to decide on team names. If a captain is absent, the other captain can appoint, with teacher approval, another team member to serve on that day.

Class Procedures and Instruction

During the first lesson, class managerial routines and safety rules should be established. Managerial and transitional routines help save time that can be used for instruction and practice. Rigorously enforced safety rules are especially important for gymnastics. A typical class entry routine is for students to come into the gym dressed appropriately, remove their shoes and socks, place any jewelry, money, or other items in their shoes, and find their own space on team mats. (Each team has mat space that is its "home.")

Once at their mats, captains should get warm-ups started immediately. Warming up is important both physically and mentally to get students on task and prepare them for the lesson. Warm-up routines can easily be made more efficient by taping cues (or music with dubbed cues) on a cassette tape. Captains take attendance, report it to the teacher, then lead the warm-up. A cued-cassette warm-up also lets you

Captain's Contract

Team name _____   Sport _____

Grade _____   Homeroom teacher _____

A captain should lead by example in the following areas:

Areas:

1. Good sport behavior.
2. Fair play—know and play by class and game rules.
3. Cooperation—whenever possible, team decisions should be made democratically.
4. Hard work—practice and work your hardest to be a good team player, as well as a good team leader. Stress and compliment your team on the well-played game, rather than only the game won.
5. Respect—teammates, other classmates, officials, teachers, and equipment.
6. Positive attitude—work positively with others to encourage them to try and not to be afraid to mess up.
7. Responsibility—turn in lineups and perform duties responsibly.

Duties:

1. Team warm-up and attendance.
2. Be sure all team members have partner or group to work with before you start to work.
3. Help team members in a positive way who need your assistance.
4. Be sure that equipment is safely and properly set up and used.
5. Safety is of utmost importance! Report any flagrant violations of rules or unsafe situations to teacher immediately.
6. Turn in all lineups, etc., on time.

Captains' signatures _____ and _____

We, the undersigned team members, will work together as a team, following the rules and our captains:

_____   _____

_____   _____

_____   _____

_____   _____

_____   _____

Figure 4.1   This captain's contract provides specific duties and general areas of responsibility.

circulate more freely to give support and feedback to students. Safety rules need to be reviewed at the outset of each lesson. Lessons should end with a closing routine, geared toward cooling down, settling students, and review.

The early part of the season is devoted to learning the skills to be used in the initial competition—the compulsory competition—which provides children an immediate goal to work toward. Any of the gymnastics events for women or men can be modified and introduced at this level. The events in this chapter were chosen based on the experience of students in K-3 physical education: rocking/rolling, static/dynamic balance, absorbing force in landings, hanging/swinging/climbing, body shapes, locomotor and nonlocomotor skills, and weight transfer on different body parts. In the third grade, students were first introduced to basic gymnastics skills.

Student Roles

Students learn to be gymnastic performers, spotters, and spectators. Some students will gain experience as captains. All students will learn about judging gymnastic performances, but you will do the actual judging of competitions.

Captains are responsible for reporting attendance and proper dress at the start of class. Captains also lead the daily warm-up period and serve as team leaders for skill practice. They are also responsible for handing in lineups and check-off lists. Captains are their teams' first resource. They lead, demonstrate, encourage their teammates, and act as informal judges for practices.

All students also learn how to spot, including the safety issues related to both performing and spotting. When teaching spotting you also have a good opportunity to teach children to be supportive of teammates and to provide accurate skill-related feedback.

Gymnastics spectators should learn to be appreciative of good performance and to applaud it. Spectators also can root for their own teams, as long as such behavior is solely in support of their own teammates, rather than directed against gymnasts from other teams.

Competitions

The gymnastic season is composed of two competitions: a compulsory competition where all children participate in developing and performing a routine and an optional competition where children choose from among several performance options, develop their own routines, and then perform them. In the model described in this chapter, compulsory competition focuses on floor exercise routines. For the optional competitions, children choose among tumbling, balance beam, and parallel bars.

The Compulsory Competition

Floor exercise skills can be used for a compulsory competition; however, a similar format can be used to introduce other events. A compulsory floor exercise routine is introduced. Captains are used as demonstrators with teams on their home mats. Skills are demonstrated with good form, and appropriate performance technique is explained as each skill is shown. Emphasis is placed on performing the routine as it is written, because it is compulsory, not optional. Videotapes can be used to show skills and spotting techniques where appropriate. Videotapes are quite useful for absent students or for students who need extra help. Tapes also can be available daily for student use during practice. Due to differences in entry-level skills, compulsory competition should be organized by at least two skill levels. I typically use a "green" and "blue" competition, representing different levels of difficulty (see Figure 4.2 for a sample compulsory routine).

After the skills are introduced, the appropriate gymnastics etiquette and judging procedures are presented (see Figure 4.3). As teams practice, they work in partners and use skill checklists (see Figure 4.4) to monitor their progress. Eventually, each student will compete, with the approval of the teacher, at the level determined by their progress on the skill checklist. Captains are responsible for turning in the order of performance for their team in the two competitions.

Once the compulsory routine is demonstrated, the individual skills and progressions are taught, followed by concentrated practice on routines. Team members work with partners, using the checklist. While one performs, the other acts as coach, judge, and spotter (when appropriate). Skills are presented and practiced in a progressive manner. Students must receive a + rating on the checklist to move on. Skill substitutions can be made for students with strength, weight, or disability problems. I use skill posters for each event. These posters show the safety rules for that skill, performance cues, progressions, and spotting techniques. Posters are resources for captains and their teams during team practices (see Figure 4.5).

Subsequent class sessions are spent learning and refining the compulsory routine. Captains are responsible for handing out and collecting skill checklists, as well as for helping team members with problems. As practice progresses, skills are made into sequences and rehearsal of the routine becomes the dominant focus. As the compulsory competition

Gymnastic Compulsory Routine Partner Checksheet

Name _____   Homeroom teacher _____

Check system:
-   Must have a heavy spot, falls, or performs with large/medium error
+   Can perform skill, but has small form error
⊕   Perfect performance

Partner who is checking should put his initials beside his mark.
Check in pencil, so changes can easily be made as student improves.

Blue routine		Green routine	
1. Acknowledge the judge		1. Acknowledge the judge	
2. Straight body stretch		2. Straight body stretch	
3. Step forward into a lunge (hold 3 cts)		3. Step forward into a lunge (hold 3 cts)	
4. Forward roll to stand: A. On incline mat		4. Cartwheel to lunge	
B. On a flat mat			
5. Tripod balance (hold 3 cts) Feet down to stretch stand		5. Headstand (hold 3 cts) Feet down to stretch stand	
6. Chassé		6. Chassé	
7. Pivot one half turn on balls of feet		7. Pivot one half turn on balls of feet	
8. Back roll to straddle out: A. On incline mat		8. Back roll to stand	
B. On flat mat			
9. Straight jump		9. Jump one half turn	
10. Knee lunge (hold 3 cts)		10. Knee lunge (hold 3 cts)	
11. Stand—stretch to end		11. Stand—stretch to end	
12. Acknowledge the judge		12. Acknowledge the judge	

Figure 4.2 Compulsory routines at two levels of difficulty shown on a checklist for partner evaluation.

Compulsory Judging Procedures

1. The value of a perfect routine is 10.0.
   Judging is done on a deduction basis. Each performer begins with the score of 10.0 before the routine starts.
2. Deductions are made for each error/fault in form, incorrect body position, or amplitude.
3. Deductions
   a. Small errors result in a deduction of .10 to .20 points.
      Examples are toes not pointed, extra step or hop, failure to hold a static position for the required time, extra step on landing, turns not on balls of feet, or an extra pause/stop.
   b. Medium errors result in a deduction of .30 to .40 points.
      Examples are a slight touch on the mat with one or both hands in loss of balance, legs or body bent when they should be straight, a captain or teammate signals to a performer, an incomplete turn, or very low jumps.
   c. Large/serious errors result in a deduction of .50 points.
      Examples are a fall on the knees or seat, a support/fall onto one or both hands, a spotter has to touch a performer to prevent a fall, or a captain/teammate talks to a performer.
   d. Omission of a compulsory skill or not memorizing the routine can result in a deduction of up to 1.00 point.

Figure 4.3 Judging procedures for the compulsory competition.

approaches, captains act as judges for mock performances, providing feedback and encouragement to team members. Captains are responsible for submitting their team's competition order to the teacher, with captains competing first. Captains draw straws or toss coins to see which team will compete first.

One team competes at a time, and captains compete first. After competing, one captain becomes responsible for coaching and spotting the other team members as they compete while the second captain is responsible to warm up and prepare the on-deck and in-the-hole competitors. Meanwhile, other team members are spectators. Alternate teams can either act as spectators or continue to practice in other areas under the leadership of their captains.

Each competitor is judged (see Figure 4.6). It is tremendously beneficial to videotape performances. This allows you to judge performances outside of class time, and it allows students to review their performances. It also allows you to monitor the entire gym for safety procedures as students compete. When one team finishes its performances, the next team rotates to the performance setting. Scoring for the meet

Partner Checklist—Compulsory Floor Routine

Student's name: _____ *Larry L.* _____   Class: _____ *Brown 5* _____

Partner who is judging: _____ *Jack Y.* _____   Team: _____ *Twisters* _____

Check system:

+ Good performance, spotting not needed

√ Needs to work on small/medium form errors

− Much improvement needed to correct large form errors, needs a heavy spot

Blue routine	Mark	Green routine	Mark
1. Acknowledge the judge	+	1. Acknowledge the judge	+
Step forward to lunge, arms high, hold for 3 cts	+	Step forward to lunge, arms high, hold for 3 cts	+
2. Forward roll on flat mat to stand, arms high	+	2. Forward roll on flat mat to stand, arms high	√
3. Tripod balance, hold 3 cts, stand	+	3. Headstand, hold 3 cts, stand	√
4. Chassé, arms sideward	+	4. Chassé, arms sideward	+
5. Pivot one half turn, arms high	+	5. Pivot one half turn, arms high	+
6. Back roll on incline mat, stand, arms high	+	6. Back roll to stand, arms high	+
7. Straight jump, "stick" the landing	√	7. Jump one half turn, "stick" the landing	+
8. Knee lunge, arms high, hold 3 cts	+	8. Stretched stand, arms high, hold 3 cts	√
9. Stretched stand, arms high Acknowledge judge before walking off mat	+	9. Stretched stand, arms high Acknowledge judge before walking off mat	+

Figure 4.4   Completed partner checklist for compulsory routine practice.

Lunge

Hold for 3 counts

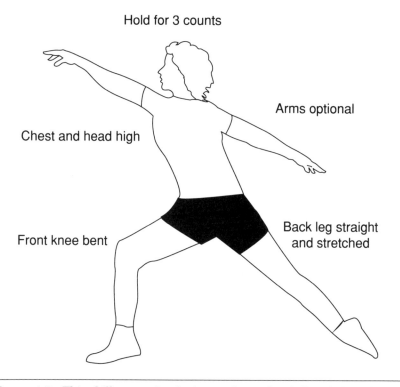

Arms optional

Chest and head high

Front knee bent

Back leg straight
and stretched

Figure 4.5   This skill poster for the lunge shows the skill and identifies
the critical performance elements.

is done in two ways. Places are totaled within levels so that within-
level awards can be given. Team totals from all competitions are then
compiled by the number of students participating and completing
routines.

The Optional Competition

The initial class session after the compulsory meet is devoted to intro-
ducing optional skills and routines. The same instruction and practice
format is used. Optional competition can include as many events as
are in the course of study depending on space and equipment constraints. The optional competition also works better when teachers
have some experience in the included events. The format shown here
includes tumbling, balance beam, and parallel bars.

Individual Compulsory Judging Form

Student's name: _____James S._____   Class: _____Brown 5_____

Beginning score = 10.00

Skill	Value	Deductions
1. Lunge–hold 3 cts	1.0	.1 Arms high
2. Forward roll	1.0	.2 Keep head tucked
3. Headstand–3 cts	1.0	.2 Balance, hold for 3 cts
4. Chassé	1.0	—
5. Pivot 1/2 turn	1.0	—
6. Back roll	1.0	.2 Push over head by straightening arms more quickly
7. Jump 1/2 turn	1.0	.1 Height
8. Knee lunge–3 cts	1.0	—
9. Etiquette	1.0	.2
10. Memorize routine	1.0	—

Total deductions = 1.0

Final score = 9.0

Comments: Nice routine, good job of flowing from one skill to another.

Figure 4.6   A compulsory routine judged using the form.

For each event there is an order of skills for which students must make choices to create their own routines (see Figure 4.7). These are presented to students on worksheets which will also be used as judging forms. For example the balance beam worksheet and judging form might include such skills as a beginning balance, travel forward, turn, static balance, travel to side, and dismount. Team members then choose the skill within each of those categories that they will use to create their routine. Students can include only those skills they have mastered based on the checklist system.

In subsequent classes, students create optional routines. Teams must ensure that they have members in each optional competition. Students make a record of their routine for themselves and for the teacher. For these sessions, the gym is set up with stations representing various events. Teams rotate among stations. When a team is assigned to an event station, members who have chosen that event practice while teammates act as judges and coaches.

The optional meet is conducted similarly to the compulsory meet. The main difference is that the optional meet proceeds by event rather than by team. Captains are responsible for turning in a list of team members that compete in each event. For example, if the beam competition is first, all students from various teams compete. This can be

Optional Balance Beam Routine
Judging Sheet

Student's name: _____ Team: _____

Class: _____

Beginning score = 10.00

Order skill	Value	Deductions
1. Acknowledge judge	*	
2. Beginning balance _____	1.0	
Travel forward _____	1.0	
Turn _____	1.0	
Static balance _____	1.0	
Travel forward/side _____	1.0	
Jump or leap _____	1.0	
Skill of choice _____	1.0	
Dismount _____	1.0	
Acknowledge judge	*	
Meet etiquette	1.0	
Routine design/memorization	1.0	

Comments: Total deductions = _____

                                               Final score = _____

Figure 4.7   Optional routine judging sheet for the balance beam competition.

followed by a parallel bars competition, then a tumbling competition. Scoring is similar to the compulsory meet.

The optional meet can be the culminating event for the season. I have used noontime recesses to conduct interclass optional meets immediately following the season. I sometimes also have taken the last day to do a gymnastics-oriented obstacle course where performance rather than time determines winners. Each part of the course is set up as a challenge. Captains take their teams through each part. For example, three floor beams can be set in a *N* formation with a goal that requires students to move safely in a different direction on each beam. Completing the task without a fall earns 20 points; completing with one fall, 10 points; completing with two falls, 5 points.

Team Points and Awards

Teachers should include in the overall point system all behaviors and performances for which they want to hold students accountable. I like to give a teamwork award based on team points for wearing proper attire, captains' leading warm-ups and reporting attendance properly, team members being on task for each lesson, finding a partner quickly, encouraging each other, and competing and practicing fairly (see Figure 4.8).

Points can also be awarded for participation and performance in meets. One point can be earned for each routine performed up to a maximum of 10. Five points can be earned for first place in each level of event, four for second, three for third, two for fourth and fifth, and one for places six through eight. I also include 1 to 10 points for each team for upholding fair play, being ready to compete, and being supportive spectators. I usually give meet awards at the conclusion of competitions, most often paper ribbons or certificates that indicate score and place in the meet. All students who participate earn awards. If there are more than eight competitors, participation awards are given.

A captain's award is given to all students who complete the responsibilities of the captain's contract. I like to give a fair play award to one team member, voted by all class members, who best displays good attitudes toward other students and competition.

Incorporating Other Gymnastics Activities

There is no need for a lack of specialized equipment to prevent physical educators from doing gymnastics sport education. If the only equipment available is mats, a tumbling and floor exercise unit can be developed.

An even more exciting and challenging alternative is acrosport, which combines group balances and floor exercises. The sport education model is ideal for acrosport. Team members can participate in single and partner balances, followed by trio or small group balances or routines. The culminating event could be a team designed balance in which single, dual, and small group balances are arranged together to create a team picture. These performances can be photographed and displayed in the gym, halls, or students' rooms. Local newspapers are always grateful for such pictures, which are usually published and create a favorable image of sport education.

Rhythmic gymnastics is another activity that is fairly undemanding of equipment. Ribbons, balls, clubs, hoops, and ropes can be used by students to perform either compulsory routines or to create their own. Rhythmic gymnastics is a great way to combine manipulative skills with floor exercise routines. Mats are the only gymnastics equipment needed to do rhythmic gymnastics.

Additional Options

The season described here is based primarily on scheduled class time. Many other opportunities exist, however, to extend that time and

Gymnastics Teamwork Award

Captains: _____

Team members: _____

_____

_____

_____

Mrs. Bell
_____
Mrs. Bell, Riverside Physical Education

February, 1993

Figure 4.8   Teamwork award given to the team earning the highest number of points based on various teamwork categories.

thereby expand what can be accomplished during the season. Unscheduled time before school, recess times, and after-school time might be available, depending on local conditions. These times can be used for team practices or for extra competitions. Written tests can be given as take home exams with teams winning points if all members pass. Writing the optional routine might become a writing assignment for homeroom.

As students mature and gain more experience with gymnastics sport education, you can add more difficulty levels to competitions, thus accommodating a wider range of abilities. Routines can become more sophisticated. Students can also learn to judge competitions themselves. USA Gymnastics Junior Olympic compulsory routines might even be used.

Teaching a Risk Sport

You are responsible for the safety of your students, and this responsibility cannot be delegated. Only activities that are included in the approved course of study should be taught. Skills should be selected that fit students' developmental characteristics and skill backgrounds. Skills should be sequenced progressively to ensure that students are not put at risk by moving forward too quickly into difficult skills. Safety rules must be taught and consistently enforced. The class must be adequately supervised.

Safety procedures are of the utmost importance. They need to be taught, prompted frequently, and visibly reinforced with posters. Prior to the unit, a notice should be sent home to parents informing them of the proper attire, safety rules, and events and equipment that students will use. Parents should be encouraged to discuss this with their children and encourage safe participation. If necessary, parents could sign and return a consent form prior to their child's participation.

USA Gymnastics is an excellent resource and educational organization. It offers safety certification, posters, publications, videotapes, and workshops. Its address is USA Gymnastics, Pan American Plaza, Ste. 300, 201 S. Capitol Ave., Indianapolis, IN 46225.

Sport Education in the Elementary Curriculum

Jane Darnell
Olde Sawmill Elementary

In this chapter I describe how sport education can be implemented as a total curriculum model at the elementary level. I discuss choice of activities, procedures for class organization, scheduling, and strategies for working with students. The examples are from a suburban K-5 school, with 50-min class periods that meet every four days on a rotating basis. The K-2 program focuses on basic skills from a movement-education perspective.

Sports and level: soccer, volleyball, basketball, gymnastics, and track and field; upper elementary grades

Seasonal format: fitness unit followed by five sport education seasons

Team format: three teams per class; stay together for school year

Competition formats: modified games, tournaments, meets

Student roles: performer, captain, referee, scorekeeper, judge

Performance records: Individual and team performance, managerial and instructional participation point system

Special features: all sport award, multiple awards, student notebooks, videotaping, performances at assemblies

---

Curricular Format and Choice of Sports

The initial activity of the year is a fitness unit that serves all the purposes of fitness and allows me to refresh my memory of returning students and learn new students' skill levels. The remainder of the school year is divided into five sport education seasons. If your elementary school requires physical education grades, then it is efficient for end of season to coincide with end of grading period. The five seasons provide sufficient class sessions to achieve goals of sport education. Schools where physical educators meet their children more frequently could maintain season length but include more than five sports per year.

Sports should be chosen that fulfill the goals of a district graded course of study. I have chosen soccer, basketball, volleyball, track and field, and gymnastics. Table 5.1 features the benefits of each sport and shows why they were chosen to provide a well-rounded sport education for children.

These five sports are repeated each year in Grades 3-5. In different situations, it might be possible to do different sports each year or to do a set rotation of sports in two grade levels with a different set of sports in the final year of elementary school. The repetition of sport seasons allows for students to make substantial progress. In gymnastics, the focus for each season changes somewhat from more formal, Olympic gymnastics skills, such as beams and floor exercises to acrosport (see page 58). In track and field, focus can change because of the large number of activities within the sport.

Selection of Teams and Captains

During the initial fitness unit, I observe all students and begin to divide them into three teams per class. Taking into account all sports in the program, I try to form teams that will allow for even competition throughout the school year. Teams also should be balanced in terms of students with leadership skills. Teams should have equal numbers of boys and girls, to the extent that class composition allows. I try to separate students who might have problems if they were on the same team. I may consult students as advisors on team selection.

An alternative method is to allow students who are highly skilled and responsible to pick three teams of equal ability without including themselves. They then can draw straws to determine team assignment. It is important that students understand that such deliberations are confidential and shouldn't be discussed with classmates.

Team membership can be changed during the school year, but this should not be done except for compelling reasons. Team membership will inevitably create some conflicts and concerns, but helping students

Table 5.1   Benefits of Sports Chosen for the Elementary Curriculum

Soccer

- Emphasizes manipulating an object with the feet
- Utilizes strategies and rules common to field invasion games, such as field hockey, football, lacrosse, and speedball
- Requires little equipment
- Involves a great deal of physical activity
- Is increasingly available as a recreational sport
- Can be played indoors or outdoors
- Is an important international sport

Basketball

- Emphasizes manipulating an object with the hands
- Utilizes strategies and rules common to court invasion games, such as team handball
- Is widely played in recreational settings
- Is an important international sport
- Can be played indoors or outdoors
- Was invented in United States
- Requires little equipment besides backboards and balls

Volleyball

- Emphasizes striking skills with hands and arms
- Utilizes strategies and rules common to divided court games, such as tennis and badminton
- Is widely played in recreational settings
- Was developed in the United States
- Requires little equipment
- Can be played indoors or outdoors

Track and field

- Accommodates a wide variety of skills and interests
- Suitable for children of various body types
- Utilizes skills universally pursued by children, such as running, jumping, and throwing

(continued)

Table 5.1   *(continued)*

Track and field *(continued)*

- Allows for competition against standards and previous best performances as well as competition against others
- Can contribute to both strength fitness and aerobic fitness
- Is an important international sport

Gymnastics

- Emphasizes total body assembly and inversion
- Requires upper body strength for many skills
- Is a form sport with a high aesthetic content
- Allows for competition against standards as well as competition against others
- Is an important international sport

work through these conflicts and resolve their concerns is important for personal development.

Two captains are elected or assigned each season for each team. Captains have a lot to do, and two students are often needed. The cocaptain can also take over when the captain is absent or when the team is divided into two areas for practice or competition. Captains are also invaluable when the teacher is absent and a substitute teacher is present.

Team members choose captains each season with the provision that no student may repeat until all students have been captain. In this text, there are many approaches to choosing captains. Being a captain is an important responsibility and should be taken seriously by all students. When students first become captains they often need guidance and support. Some are too shy, or some are too assertive. You can help them learn appropriate leadership skills.

Team Procedures and Instruction

Teams and captains form the structural basis for the physical education program for the entire school year. It is important, however, that you teach and enforce good class management routines so that as much time as possible can be devoted to sport education goals. I use the fitness unit to teach class managerial routines that will be used throughout the school year. Routines for entering the gym, transitioning between activities, equipment, and the like are taught and practiced. It is through teaching and enforcing these routines that students learn that (a) physical education is a time for learning, (b) time is limited and should not be wasted, and (c) staying on task is important. Class rules for behavior are also taught during the fitness unit.

Students stay on their teams throughout the school year. This fosters team spirit and cohesiveness. When teams are first formed, their initial decisions focus on a team name, team colors, and captains for the first sport season. Because new captains are chosen every sport season, every child will eventually be a captain sometime during the school year. I like to take team pictures early in the initial sport season and place them on bulletin boards. Students can purchase copies at minimal cost, and some of the proceeds are used to purchase awards.

Teams have a home base for each sport season where they go when they enter the gym and start with their first activity. This might be a mat space for gymnastics season, a home field for soccer season, or a home basket for basketball season. Warm-ups and initial skill practice is typically done by each team in its home area.

Each sport education season develops in a similar way. Skills and strategies are introduced and practiced, with teams working together and captains playing leadership roles. Some kind of practice event, such as a practice gymnastics competition or practice soccer game, typically precedes formal competition. As formal competition approaches, teams refine their strategies and organize themselves for competition. Because small-sided games are used, teams most often have to organize miniteams from among their total team membership. As competition progresses, more class time is devoted to it and practice time is gradually reduced.

I have developed student notebooks for each sport season. They take time to develop, but once completed are an invaluable aid. Each notebook contains information related to the technical and strategic aspects of a sport, as well as its rules. Notebooks also contain places where students complete assignments, such as to develop an optional routine in gymnastics. Students use their notebooks during class. They must keep them in good shape and return them promptly to earn teamwork points toward the all sport award. Suggested items to include in the notebook are

- information and pictures or drawings of skills;
- information and drawings of offensive and defensive strategies;
- forms for entering competitions;
- forms for practicing skills (checkoff sheets);
- a copy of the overall point system for the sport season;
- reminders of fair play suggestions (dos and don'ts); and
- any outside or homework assignments related to a sport season.

I always schedule one free day between seasons. If weather or unpredictable events cause schedule changes within a season, the extra day allows for catch-up. This is important because children get very involved in their sport season and want it to play out to the end. If the schedule goes as planned, the free day is used to do new games and group initiatives, with the team that earned the most points toward the all sport award for that season picking the activities.

Student Roles

Student roles learned and practiced in the sport education curriculum are those of performer, captain, referee, scorekeeper, and judge. As in all sport education models, captains are important for the success of the sport season. Captains have to set examples for their teams, demonstrate fair play, respect safety rules, and be on task with good behavior. Captains are also responsible for assisting with instruction and practice, especially during early stages of each sport season. They also organize their teams, make decisions about player combinations, and manage their teams throughout the season. Captains also have managerial duties such as checking attendance, reporting improper dress and tardiness, assisting with equipment, and handing in competition assignments. I have captains sign a contract that explains their responsibilities. Fulfillment of the contract leads to a special award at the end of the season. Examples of captain's contracts can be seen on pages 39 and 49.

The three-team concept is important to the way I implement sport education. In many sports, it allows two teams to compete while one team is responsible for refereeing and scorekeeping. The third team is called a duty team. Because sport education typically utilizes small-sided, timed competitions, no team occupies the duty team position for an extended period of time. For example, let's say that in volleyball season we are having a 3 vs. 3 competition. Each team of 8 to 11 students has to field two or three 3-person teams. Games last for 6 to 8 min and start and stop together. In one game time, four 3 vs. 3 games are being played between two of the three class teams. The third class team supplies referees and scorekeepers for those games. When that game time is over, the duty team becomes a competitive team and one of the competitive teams rotates to duty team for the next game time. Once students learn the rotation among competing and duty team responsibilities, transitions between competitions go quite quickly as students move to their assigned places and prepare themselves for their next roles.

When students regularly referee and keep scores and statistics, they learn rules and recognize performance in ways that are far more accountable than merely writing answers on tests. I also have learned that students gain a better respect for officials and behave better towards them when they have occupied that role themselves.

Competitions

The competitions throughout the sport education curriculum are varied. The soccer competition is actually a series of competitions beginning with 1 vs. 1 and culminating with a minisoccer tournament (see pages 40-43). The gymnastics competitions, compulsory and optional, are described on pages 50-57. Track and field competition can be arranged either through individuals' points for performance based on standards for each event (e.g., a student would earn a certain number of points for jumping a particular height, jumping a particular distance, or running a certain course in a particular time), or through a more conventional competition format where teams compete in minimeets. Most of the competition formats described on pages 26-27 are adaptable to sport education in an elementary curriculum.

Most importantly, competitions are kept low key, mainly emphasizing fun and fair play. Students are always encouraged to do their best, and teammates are taught and encouraged to provide support for their companions. An appropriate view of competition is taught and reinforced. "Try hard, play fair, and celebrate the accomplishments of your classmates" is the prevailing ethic.

The Award System

The central organizing scheme of this sport education model is the all sport award. Class structures, management, and procedures all are related to team achievement in this system. The all sport award is a yearlong award given to the team that accumulates the highest percentage of points. Points are awarded in four areas (see Table 5.2). Daily teamwork points are given for warm-ups, dress and no tardies, and participation. Cognitive points are given for refereeing, notebooks, work sheets, and tests. Teams begin with 40 fair play points and get deductions if they break fair play rules. Tournament points are won by winning or tieing contests and for playing cooperatively.

Notice that point values for winning in competition are a relatively minor aspect of the all sport award. There are points so that students learn that trying hard to win is important. The award, however, typically goes to the team that works together well, does its other sport education roles well, participates completely, and plays fairly.

Notice also that penalties that result in point losses from fair play points are severe. Part of the fair play system relates to class rules. A

Table 5.2 All Sport Award Point System

Daily teamwork points: (30 possible points, 1 earned in each category on a daily basis)
 10–warm-ups/cooldowns properly completed by all team members
 10–all team members dressed appropriately and no tardies
 10–team participation in class activities

Team cognitive points: (30 possible, awarded on an all-or-none basis in each category)
 10–refereeing
 10–notebooks completed and turned in on time
 10–tests and worksheets, turned in on time, all team members get a passing grade (70 percent or better)

Fair play points: (40 initial points)
 1 point deducted for warning by teacher or referee
 2 points deducted for timeout by teacher or yellow card
 3 points deducted for repeated timeout, red card, or technical foul

Tournament points
 1 point for playing cooperatively
 1 point for each win
 1/2 point for each tie

teacher warning costs one point. A time-out costs two points. Three points are deducted for continuous off-task or disruptive behavior. During competitions, we use the yellow card/red card system. The yellow card is a warning, but a red card or a technical foul results in a three-point deduction from the fair play point total.

Figure 5.1 shows the seasonal summary scoresheet for the all sport award points. The ethic of the all sport award—"play hard, play fair, have fun"—is continually emphasized and posted in a prominent position in the gym under the all sport award.

Students like to be recognized for achieving goals. It is important to reward many different kinds of accomplishments within the sport education model. Each season produces many individual and team winners in the regular competitions: for example, winners in the 1 vs. 1, 2 vs. 2, and 3 vs. 3 soccer competitions or place and team winners in gymnastics meets. In addition to these awards, the following are also useful.

Class:

Team															
	1	2	3	1	2	3	1	2	3	1	2	3	1	2	3
Sport	Soccer			Basketball			Gymnastics			Volleyball			Track & field		
Daily team points															
Good warm-up/no tardies															
Proper dress															
Sport/Tourn. points															
Sportsmanship															
Officiating															
Tournament points															
Cognitive points															
Notebooks															
Tests															
Team totals (%)															
Cumulative total															

Figure 5.1 Seasonal summary score sheet for the all sport award.

Captain's Award—Given to all captains who complete their assigned duties in the captain's contract.

Most Improved—Each team votes for each season.

Best Sportsperson—Voted on by the class.

Teamwork Award—Given to each team member when their team earns all possible teamwork points for a season.

Fair Play Award—Given to each team member when their team earns all possible fair play points in a season.

Numerous sport-specific awards can also be awarded each season: for example, most aces, most saves, and the like. These awards are easy to manage if students have been taught to keep performance data during contests. These awards are more likely to be included in the upper grades because students are more ready to keep reliable records.

The Impact of Sport Education

The gymnasium can become a colorful, festive facility in sport education. Skill posters can be used to remind children of the technical elements of performance for each sport. Seasonal and yearlong points are posted prominently. Fair play posters remind students of class rules and expectations. Using pictures of performers selected carefully to show gender, race, and age differences for the particular sport of the season helps students realize that sport participation is not specific to age, gender, or race.

From time to time, students respond quite favorably to having important competitions videotaped. Students love to watch themselves perform. I have also used one member per team or one member per class to be responsible for write ups on the season that might appear in a school newspaper, in a special sport sheet (newsletter), or on a sports headlines (bulletin) board. Classroom teachers often look for ways to integrate activities. There are a number of ways, such as writing assignments related to specific sports being learned, keeping and calculating statistical information related to performance, or making special decorations or awards.

Sport education seasons can be successfully extended in lunchtime recess or intramural time, thus allowing for interclass competitions in all sports. It allows for variations on the sports being learned. This arrangement can be formalized so that lunchtime recess or intramural time becomes a required extension of physical education.

When children participate in sport education for several seasons or years, they become adept at organizing and implementing their own sport involvement. I recall how amazed I was several years ago when I organized an intramural floor hockey tournament as an enrichment activity (we hadn't done floor hockey in physical education). Students organized themselves into teams and volunteered for referee duties. From the first day of the tournament, teams were in the gym ahead of schedule and ready to go at the scheduled time. Captains who had been elected took charge and made sure that positions were covered. Transitions with substitutes went smoothly and without argument. All students played an equal amount of time (in accord with one of the rules). Teams frequently came to me to ask for extra practice time with the equipment. They really did a great job. It was one of those experiences where you realize that what you try to achieve sometimes does get done!

Chapters 3 through 5 have shown that sport can be taught responsibly and well to children in elementary physical education. Not only is sport education a valuable model for teaching skills and strategic play, but teachers and students alike have reported how useful the model is for teaching cooperation, fair play, and an appropriate view of competition. These valuable learning outcomes can be extended in secondary education, which is the focus of the remainder of Part II, chapters 6 through 9.

Middle School Volleyball

Jessica Hook
The Hockaday School

In this chapter I describe the efforts of a first-year teacher to implement sport education at middle school level. The effort exemplifies what has been described as the "beginner's model" (Siedentop, Mand, & Taggart, 1986). No changes were made in the physical education program to accommodate this effort, nor were any other physical education teachers involved. I simply took my own class assignments and experimented with sport education.

Sport and level: volleyball, middle school

Seasonal format: 15 class sessions, meeting daily

Team format: two teams; teacher selected

Competition format: modified tournament, culminating game

Student roles: performer, captain, cocaptain, referee, scorekeeper

Performance records: team points, skill hustle scores, competition points, skill and knowledge tests

Special features: awards, computer skill sheet

Selection of Teams and Captains

Assigning students to teams on the first day of a season is essential to deriving the full benefits of sport education. Along with their role in developing a real sense of sport play among students, teams, in my version, provide the driving force for both the managerial and instructional systems in my classes. Affiliation with a team provides both a motivation to participate vigorously and an important source of peer accountability.

I utilize a two-team model, an *AB* team and a *CD* team. The gym is set up in a grid pattern. Across the front wall of the gym, the letters *A, B, C,* and *D* are fixed at equal intervals. Extending back from each letter are numbers taped to the floor. The letter and number combinations indicate home base for each student in the class. If, for example, Traci is assigned to *B4* at the start of a season, she goes to the *B* line and then to the *4* on the floor to find her home base.

Thus far, I have assigned teams and captains. In the first sport education season of the school year students are assigned alphabetically to home bases. If the teams that result from this assignment are markedly unequal, changes are made to ensure fairer competition. Because a major focus of my classes is cooperative work among teams and skill development, rather than interteam competition, I seldom have to make many changes in home base assignments.

Class Procedures and Instruction

Each class session uses set routines that reduce management time and ensure as much learning time as possible. Students enter the gym and go to their home bases. Captains lead short (approximately 4-min) warm-ups, typically several stretches done to cadence for holding the static stretch. Captains and cocaptains then get equipment necessary for drills and distribute the equipment among their teammates.

A 6-min basic skill practice routine then follows with sufficient, continuous activity to raise the heart rate. This is an important phase of class that I call the *skill hustle*. The gym is set up in four skill-practice stations (see Figure 6.1). On signal the subteams (*A, B, C, D*) move quickly to their assigned beginning stations where they do a 1-min timed practice, with captains recording performance scores. On signal, subteams quickly move to the next stations where another 1-min skill timing occurs. This is repeated for four stations.

Each station's skills change as the season progresses. Early in the season, when skills are first introduced, I might use a zigzag line jump, a rapid wall set, a hitter's station, and a serve station. The goal at the zigzag line station is to jump from one side of the line to the other while progressing from one end to the other (and then back) as many times as possible in the 1 min. There are sufficient lines for each team member to participate at the same time. Captains record scores.

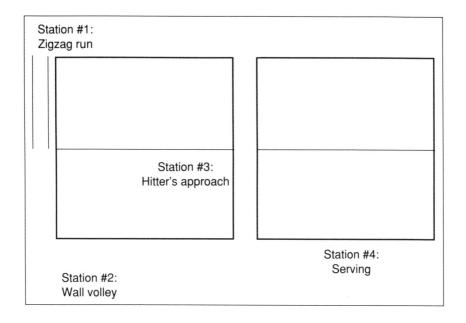

Figure 6.1 Gymnasium setup for the four-station skill hustle.

The rapid wall set has students behind a line 8 feet (2.44 m) from the wall where two parallel lines are taped with the top line 11 feet (3.35 m) off the floor (see Figure 6.2). On signal, students count the number of legal sets they can make between the wall lines in 1 min. Captains record scores.

The hitter's station is for practicing the approach and stroke for spiking (which technically is very similar to the overhand throw). As students approach this station they each pick up two knee pads and spread out across the length of a volleyball net at their *touch points*. The touch point is a mark where the players begin a three-step approach to a vertical jump without hitting the net with their bodies. Each player carries a knee pad in each hand. As they approach the net, players jump vertically, throwing both arms up in the air. If a player is a right-handed hitter, the knee pad in the left hand is dropped over the net first, while the knee pad in the right hand is thrown down over the net forcefully using the hitter's arm swing motion. Using a knee pad in the nonthrowing hand requires students to lift both arms, which is essential to good jumping. Students retrieve knee pads by running around the right side of the net and returning on the left side where they repeat the approach and throw. After 1 min, captains record scores.

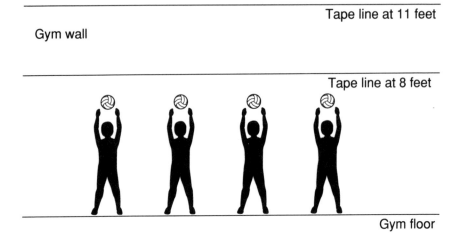

Tape line at 11 feet

Gym wall

Tape line at 8 feet

Gym floor

Figure 6.2   Diagram for the rapid wall set station.

At the serve station, students serve (over or underhand) at a distance appropriate to their skill level. They jog around the right side to retrieve and return to the other side to serve again. After 1 min, captains record scores.

Station skills change as the season progresses, and records are kept by team. At the end of the season, a computer-printed statistics sheet is given to each student. The skill hustle phase is also designed to increase the heart rate. The 1-min timing gets students going and keeps them going to try to get more opportunities for daily skill scores. Students are constantly reminded that their score is the number of successful attempts. The timing is not meant simply to reward a lot of attempts, but rather successful attempts: for example, the legal set between the lines on the wall, a successful three-step approach and hitting motion, and a successful serve.

The skill hustle phase is followed by a short review of the previous day's practice. This is followed by a 10- to 15-min introductory phase in which new skills and strategies are introduced and practiced. Most practice tasks in this phase are also "competed" among the teams, with timings and successful execution the main focus.

Even in the early stages of the season, classes end with a game activity, often a team scrimmage that focuses on skills and strategies practiced that day. These scrimmages and games are typically small-sided (3 vs. 3) with teams from one larger team practicing against teams from the other larger team. Class ends with a short review of the lesson.

Student Roles

Students learn to be volleyball performers, captains and cocaptains, referees, linespersons, and scorekeepers. Captains are assigned by home base position. For example, for the first season *A1* is assigned as captain and *B1* as cocaptain for the *AB* team, with *C1* as captain and *D1* as cocaptain for the *CD* team. This is an easy way to create two overall teams, with subdivisions of two smaller teams per larger team.

The first responsibility of captains is to name the team. For example, if the *AB* team chooses *Acers*, the name replaces the *AB* designation and that team is referred to throughout the season as the Acers. Captains and cocaptains have daily responsibilities. They lead warm-ups each day, help distribute and collect equipment, help coach in various drills, keep records during skill practice, set up team assignments for competitions, and generally ensure the smooth operation of classes by managing their teams well.

Students learn and practice refereeing and linesperson responsibilities. All students initially learn these skills during the instructional phase of daily lessons, then practice in the culminating game and scrimmage phase of the daily lesson. Just before the first major competition of the volleyball season, the main focus of one lesson becomes a 3 vs. 3 tournament, officiating, and calling lines. The practice and game phase allows each student to practice officiating.

Have the students learn and practice signals for in and out balls, calling the serve to initiate service, and point awarding. Stop scrimmages frequently to discuss rotation, scoring, and referee decisions. Students simply rotate from player positions to official positions. For officials, the importance of keeping control, keeping the game flowing, and otherwise not being conspicuous is stressed.

Competition

The entire season is a competition between the two major teams. Nearly every phase of each lesson involves some competition between the two teams for points. The formal game competition begins at the middle of the season and progresses toward the end of the season. The main competition is a 3 vs. 3 game with modified boundaries. Each team selects several three-person teams for the 3 vs. 3 tournament. A schedule of tournament play is posted.

The last day of class is devoted to a full-sided match with officials, linespersons, and substitutions. It is made very special and all of the formalities of volleyball are observed.

Team Points and Awards

The driving motivational mechanism for the sport education season is team points. All managerial, instructional, and competition efforts are part of the team points competition, which determines the volleyball champion for the season. This strategy allows me to emphasize team cooperation and skill development as strongly as winning volleyball games.

Team Points

Team points are tallied daily and posted in the gym so that students can see the progress of their teams. Some points are earned by meeting a standard, such as appropriate dress, and, thus, can be earned by all teams at the same time. Other points are competitive, such as speed of response to a teacher's signal, and can be won by only one team at a time. Managerial and behavioral issues have been integrated into the point system, as have instructional and practice performances, along with the more obvious competition results.

Managerial team points can be earned for a variety of tasks. The first team to be out of the locker room with all players on their home bases earns a point. Each team with all members in uniform earns a point. Teams always practice together, in assigned team areas, with the *AB* team on one side of the gym and the *CD* team on the other. Thus, when I blow the whistle to stop a drill or to gain attention, the team that is quiet and in control of volleyballs first can earn a point.

Instructional points are usually awarded during the main instruction and practice phase of the lesson. I try to use practice drills that have clear goals, that is, they can be timed and counted. I emphasize correct performance in the counting. Thus, if I have set up a triad drill for forearm passing, I might have a competition to see which three-person team can make consecutive, successful passes. The winning triad earns a point for its team. This team point competition is between the two larger class teams; when smaller groups compete, they always earn points for their larger team.

During the 3 vs. 3 competition, each three-person team has a chance to win points for its larger team. These points accumulate as competition progresses. I also award team points for outstanding fair play and good sporting behavior by individuals and teams. This allows me to use them as examples in class and to recognize this important behavior. The winner of the full-sided, culminating championship game is awarded a designated number of points reflecting the importance of that event in the seasonal competition.

Awards

The main award is the volleyball championship award for the team that has accumulated the most team points throughout the season. A certificate is given to each member of the winning team. I have created certificates using a computer graphics program (see Figure 6.3). These can be output directly on heavy stock certificate paper, depending on your equipment, or the output can be copied onto heavier stock.

A fair play award is also given to the individual in class who has demonstrated a willingness to help classmates, who wins and loses with grace, who plays according to the letter and spirit of the rules, and who puts the welfare of the team and class above that of her- or himself. This is an important award. Criteria for the award are made known to students and discussed with them. I make clear that the award is not based on popularity or superior skill. Students vote using a written ballot.

Captains and cocaptains receive a team captain certificate for the effort they put forth during the season. Because captains change for each season, all students gain leadership experience from being a captain sometime during the school year.

Awards are presented in front of the class following the final championship game. Each winner's name is called and they receive certificates in front of their classmates. During the awards ceremony, students also receive a computerized statistics sheet outlining their progress in various skill drills throughout the season.

Teacher Reactions and Reflections

As a beginning teacher on a large middle school physical education staff, I was able to utilize sport education in my own classes as long as I conformed to the general expectations and scheduling format of the department and school. In a sense, I was allowed to do my own thing, and it worked well. Once teams and class routines were established, a major portion of class is managed by captains and team members. Students enjoyed the affiliation of teams and they participated vigorously and enthusiastically in the team point system.

I can see, however, how much more successful the model might be if it were adopted throughout a middle school physical education department. Like most schools, teachers in our school each have their own structures. If we could establish a common sport education model, the transfer from class to class and year to year would be substantial. Students would be fully aware of the sport education format and able

Figure 6.3   Certificate given to each member of winning team in the volley-ball championship.

to take over even more responsibility for their own sport involvement. Tournaments and competitions could be expanded, and we could employ intraclass competitions as extra culminating events. The festiveness that is so important to sport education in general and middle school students in particular would be easier to develop and sustain; indeed, it would become a school-wide celebration.

CHAPTER
7

High School Touch Rugby and Tennis

Bevan Grant
University of Otago

In this chapter I describe sport education touch rugby and tennis programs at Leith High School in New Zealand. Leith High School was one of 21 New Zealand high schools that took part in a national trial of sport education with 10th grade students. Much of the material in this chapter is based on experiences of teachers in the 21 high schools, Leith High School being the main example. Sport education represented a new approach that challenged the teachers' existing beliefs and their traditional short unit, multiactivity approach to programming physical education for high school youth. The national experiment was so successful that more than 100 high schools asked for staff development to try sport education in the following school year. More than 150 high schools have now adopted the model.

Sports and level: touch rugby, tennis; high school

Seasonal format: 22 lesson season, 4 days a week

Team format: two classes combined, eight teams, student selectors

Competition format: double round-robin (touch rugby), singles and doubles (tennis)

Student roles: performer, sport board, selector, captain, coach, manager, referee, scorekeeper, publicist, trainer

Performance records: competition outcomes

Special features: notice boards, team photos, all-school culminating events, visits to local sport sites, certificates

---

Selection of Teams and Captains

Sport education was explained on the first day of the season. We took time to explain the model because it represents a departure from the regular physical education program, both for teachers and students. A first task was the election of a sports board, which would be responsible for the organization and control of events throughout the season (see page 87). The sports board is typically a group of 4 to 6 students (equal numbers of boys and girls) elected by the class after a brief discussion of what the roles entail and what kinds of students might be best suited. Team selection can be done by the sports board or it can be done by a group of student-selectors elected by classmates for the specific purpose of selecting teams that are fair and workable.

Successful team selection is crucial to the sport education season. It is imperative that teams be as equal as possible. Before selecting teams, selectors should be briefed on their responsibilities. Selectors should take into account skill levels, student interest and attitudes, social groupings within the class, gender balance, and regular absentees. Selectors should also solicit the teacher's advice.

Teachers in the New Zealand experiment reported that the fair teams ethic was guarded jealously by students, who have a keen sense of fairness and justice at high school age. Team membership is fundamentally important to the goals of sport education and selecting fair teams helps teammates get off to a good start and learn to value the contributions of each team member.

In touch rugby, modified games were used as trials by selectors to help make their decisions. During trials, students continuously played modified touch rugby games but were mixed and rotated among teams. Trials were typically preceded by a scrimmage so that game play and rules were clear to students. Trial games were self-officiated. In tennis, both skills tests and the rankings from singles competition were used by selectors to choose teams.

In touch rugby (60 students) eight teams were formed. In tennis (30 students) six teams were formed. Once teams are formed, the first item of team business is to select a coach, a captain, and a manager. Nearly every high school in the experiment chose to differentiate leadership among those roles. Each has important duties and, together, they allow for more and better leadership opportunities for students. The specific roles for these three positions for the touch rugby season are described on page 87.

Class Procedures and Instruction

Remember, the teachers in this project tried sport education for the first time. One of their concerns, at the outset, was giving over to students so much responsibility for the operation of the program. Two teachers at Leith High School combined classes for the rugby season. This created a pool of 60 students, organized into eight teams. The tennis season was done with single classes of 30 students, each organized into six teams.

After explaining the sport education model and electing a sports board, each teacher chose to begin the season with a considerable amount of direct instruction. Rules, sporting history, rituals, and other points of interest were included with basic skills and strategies for the respective sports. The lesson-by-lesson flow of the seasons is described in Tables 7.1 and 7.2. The pace of these early lessons was controlled by teachers, who communicated to students their sense of expectations for learning and their enthusiasm for the sport education model.

As the season progressed, teachers transferred to students the major responsibilities for implementation of the program. The role of teachers shifted as students took more initiative for what happened on a day-to-day basis. As teacher reflections will show, later in this chapter, the provision for student responsibility is a key educational feature of sport education.

Managers began to take over major responsibilities for daily practice and competition, from organizing equipment to making sure that team

Table 7.1 Touch Rugby Seasonal Format

Session	Activity
1	Introduce sport education, touch rugby skills, discuss and elect sports board
2	Skill practice, modified game, rules, rituals
3	Skill practice, modified game, elect selectors
4	Trials
5	Announce teams, selection of coach, captain, manager, skill practice
6	Skill and strategy practice in teams, officiating
7	Skill and strategy practice, preseason games, discuss competition format
8-14	Round-robin competition 1, one team on duty each day
15	Review round 1, discuss team needs, team practice, lunchtime games versus other classes
16-22	Round-robin competition 2, one team on duty each day
23	Festival games against other classes, awards ceremony

Table 7.2   Tennis Seasonal Format

Session	Activity
1	Introduce sport education, tennis skills, elect sports board
2-5	Skill practice: serve, forehand, backhand; history and traditions of tennis, rules, rituals, doubles play, officiating
6	Skills test: serve, forehand, backhand
7	Singles games for ranking
8	Singles games, teams selected
9	Team practices, doubles competition format explained
10-14	Doubles competition round-robin, players matched through equivalent rankings
15	Review doubles competition, singles rankings within teams
16-21	Singles competition between teams, play equivalent ranking
22	Visit local tennis center, games, awards ceremony

members were in the right places at the right times. Coaches assumed more and more responsibility for daily practice. They made sure that all students were involved, planned practice sessions based on the needs of players, led discussions of game tactics, and made substitutions during competitions. Captains worked with coaches on strategy, represented their teams for competition decisions (for example, a coin toss), interacted with referees on behalf of their teams, led the postcompetition cheer and exchange with opponents, and generally set the role model for fair play within the context of the sport.

The touch rugby program utilized the concept of the duty team, a feature that was widely used with great success throughout the New Zealand experiment. The duty team does not compete for the day or portion of the lesson that it is on duty. The duty team is responsible for organizing game equipment before and after class, making sure all teams are in the right location for competition, starting and stopping games on time, collecting and recording competition results, providing the referees for all contests, providing the scorers and timekeepers, and reporting any problems to the sports board. Each day of the round-robin competition, a different team had duty responsibilities.

Student Roles

Students learned to be tennis and rugby performers, referees, captains, coaches, managers, scorekeepers, publicists, and trainers. The number of responsible positions on each team was quite important to the outcomes reported by teachers, because holding positions of responsibility that affect the overall welfare of the team throughout the sport season caused students to take their roles seriously.

The sports board was responsible for the organization and control of events throughout the season. Duties of sports boards included

- planning the competitions with the teacher;
- dealing with disputes or student requests;
- meeting with the teacher to share ideas and feedback from students;
- providing positive role models for teams;
- planning the culminating event; and
- ensuring the smooth day-to-day functioning of the program.

Whether playing touch rugby or tennis, managers, coaches, and captains had specific roles, which are described below.

The manager duties were to

- support the coach;
- organize equipment for team practice;
- ensure that players know who, where, and when they are playing;
- check for appropriate uniforms, numbers, and so forth;
- arrange for substitutes for absent players;
- report concerns to coach and teacher;
- organize the team when it is on duty.

The coach duties were to

- be fair to all players on their team;
- involve all players in practice and competition;
- listen to ideas of players;
- plan active practices, seek advice of teacher;
- discuss ideas with manager and captain;
- make substitutions during contests.

The captain duties were to

- liaise with coach relative to practice and game strategies;
- make on-court or on-field decisions for team;
- represent the team to referee during competition;
- lead team in congratulations and postcompetition rituals;
- be an example of fair play.

Some schools specified that each team had to elect a trainer who would be responsible for a first-aid kit and familiar with the likely injuries in their sport and how to treat them. Some schools utilized team publicists who kept notice boards up to date and generally publicized their teams' efforts throughout the school using posters, newspaper articles, and the like.

Officiating was taught as a regular part of early season skills and knowledge focus. All students learned to officiate the sport being played and officiated during regular competitions. Team captains and coaches have particular responsibilities to model appropriate behavior toward officials and to ensure that their teams play fairly and respect officials' decisions.

Teams can specify publicists from among their ranks or this can be the responsibility of the sports board. Most schools developed a special notice board that was reserved for sport education news and notices. Competition schedules, game results, rules, duty team tasks, team photos, and posters about the sport were the items most typically posted on notice boards.

Seasonal Competition

Tables 7.1 and 7.2 show the seasonal format, including competitions, for touch rugby and tennis. Both competitions were organized by teams. The touch rugby season was centered on two round-robin tournaments. The tennis competition began with a team doubles round-robin competition, followed by a team singles round-robin tournament. In most cases in the New Zealand experiment, teachers used trial contests and preseason scrimmages prior to formal competitions. Much teaching was done in these sessions. Because students were on teams and preparing for competitions, they tended to take practice sessions seriously. In each season, time was taken between the two major competitions to assess performance and make decisions about the next competition. There were also days when competition did not take place, and the class focused on extended skill or strategy development, discussed competition issues, or learned more about the sport via some teaching aid such as a video of a regional, national, or international competition.

In both touch rugby and tennis, a special culminating event was organized by the sports boards. The touch rugby boards organized interclass competitions that were all-school events, complete with all the festivities that surround major rugby competitions. These final games were followed by an awards ceremony. The culminating event in tennis was a visit to a local tennis facility where games were played and awards presented. One purpose for choosing the tennis culminating event was to have students experience how tennis is played in the community at a local tennis club.

The sports board takes over major responsibility for competitions, but is advised by the teacher. Experiences of teachers suggest that successful competition formats address the following issues:

- Clearly defined rules that promote full participation
- Modified rules and equipment to ensure a friendly game
- Short, commonly timed (start and stop) games
- Clear schedules and posted results
- Appropriate scoring systems
- Emphasis on fair play, even to the point of including it in the scoring system
- Emphasis on good officiating and acceptance of decisions

Awards

Awards were presented on the final day of the season. The kinds and numbers of awards used in the New Zealand experiment were many and varied. Typically, there was a team championship award, fair play awards, and recognition for sports board members, captains, coaches, and managers. In some schools, each player got a certificate commemorating his or her participation in the sport season. In some schools, tokens of appreciation (such as for soft drinks) were presented to members of winning teams.

In New Zealand, grades are not given for physical education in the same way as is typically done in the United States. Thus it was not common for teachers in the New Zealand project to devise and use point systems that are useful when teachers need to report grades. An example of a secondary school point system leading to grades can be found on page 109.

Teacher Reactions and Reflections

Teachers quickly moved from their in-control mode to one in which they were supportive and available but had backed off from an authoritarian role to one of facilitator. At the outset, this was difficult for most teachers in the New Zealand experiment, but at the end it proved to be the most widely respected and valued outcome of the experience.

Teachers found that team coaches and captains actually sought their help in identifying strategies and helping to solve skill problems. Many teachers regularly interacted with teams about their progress, serving as an additional advisor. It was important, however, not to identify with one team more than another and to be equally available to all teams.

Affiliation with the team and the interactive nature of being responsible for their own sport season quickly produced a large number of diverse interactions among teammates. Not all of these were positive! Teachers found it difficult to avoid intervening immediately, but they quickly discovered that teams could work out problems and that the process produces valuable educational experiences for students. Teachers reported that they learned to recognize when to back off and when to intervene.

> *Initially I found it quite hard to get away from my dictatorial approach. I got frustrated by this and started to interfere. I actually got told to "back off" by one of the teams. I could see them making mistakes and they didn't want me to help them . . . Their case was eventually proved by their vast improvement in skills. . . . Their willingness to be part of a group with a purpose was so evident. This opportunity really heightened their concentration so the quality of their learning versus time involved would have been better than in normal physical education time.*
>
> —Secondary PE teacher

There is little doubt that sport education is a student-centered model and that teachers quickly move off the center-stage role they are accustomed to playing. Although teachers may be less visible than when at center stage, their guidance, leadership, and facilitation is necessary for the success of the model. Teachers reported that their role as facilitators helped them to achieve a new and more satisfying relationship with their students.

There is no doubt that the initial experience with the sport education model challenged the beliefs of many New Zealand high school physical educators, including the teachers at Leith High School.

> *Sport education certainly blew apart some of my long-term theories about using sport in physical education. I was skeptical about this at first but I've now seen what it can do.*
>
> —Leith High School PE teacher

> *Sport education was a real mountain [challenge] from the start, and to see it go through and generate the enthusiasm it did was quite worthwhile.*
>
> —Leith High School PE teacher

Teachers at Leith and throughout New Zealand were consistent in what they reported as the positive benefits of sport education. They saw students apply themselves more responsibly and consistently than was typical in the teacher-directed, multiactivity format. They saw signs of skillful play that were, in their judgment, more advanced than typical. Quite importantly, they reported that lower-skilled students played valuable roles on teams and profited markedly from their experiences. The affiliation with teams and the preparation for competition lent a seriousness to daily sessions that previously had been absent.

More than any other, however, surprise was the consistent reaction, sometimes nearing amazement, that 10th graders could take over major responsibilities for the sport education season and perform them so well.

One of the reasons I think it was so positive was a shift from win, win, win to looking at a whole range of behaviors like coaching, umpiring, managing, being a captain, being on duty, being a spectator, and so on . . . the students liked the competition but also wanted to learn something in depth about tennis. This program put a whole new light on sport and how it really is an important part of physical education.

—Leith High School PE teacher

The three teachers at Leith, like their counterparts throughout New Zealand, claim that their previous efforts with a multiactivity program could not achieve the level of meaning attached to these types of outcomes. As a result, sport education has now become a permanent and important part of their physical education programs.

High School Fitness Applications

Deborah Tannehill
The Ohio State University

The sport education model can easily accommodate fitness activities. The strength training program I describe in this chapter was developed by a high school physical education teacher (Sweeney, Tannehill, & Teeters, 1992). The running and aerobics applications have a cardiovascular focus but utilize the sport education model. The range of applications in this chapter provide sufficient information to develop other applications using free weights, exercise machines, or partner work.

Strength Training

Because research has shown an increasing number of benefits of strength training in children, more experts encourage the activity than ever before. These benefits include increasing muscular strength and endurance, preventing injuries, and improving performance in sports and recreational activities. When you teach strength training, it is important to motivate students by interesting them in physical fitness. It also is important to set realistic expectations and goals.

> *Sport and level:* strength training, high school
>
> *Seasonal format:* twenty-four class sessions, meeting three times weekly
>
> *Team format:* weight divisions, class selected captains, blind draw or auction for team selection
>
> *Competition formats:* weekly challenges, individual competitions, team competitions
>
> *Student roles:* performer, captain, judge, scorer, publicist
>
> *Performance records:* individual records, technique judging, team records
>
> *Special features:* individual awards, team awards, best technique awards

Selection of Teams and Captains

The team format, whether for mixed or single-gender classes, should be organized by weight divisions. The specific application used here was for a class of 31 girls, ages 14 to 18. The season began by having the class select seven captains. Four weight divisions were created based on the range of weights (in pounds) in the particular class: the *A* division (96-106), *B* division (112-119), *C* division (121-134), and *D* division (more than 135).

Teams can be selected in several ways. One way is to have a blind draw in which captains draw one student name from the students in each of the divisions. A second method is to pretest students on selected events, such as the incline press, bench press, squat, and clean. You then rate students based on pretests, with each rating worth a certain number of points. Captains are allotted 100 points to select team members by bidding, which forces captains to consider students' potential to improve and ways to optimize team performance across the weight divisions. Although this might appear to be an inappropriate pick-and-choose method, students do this objectively and it seems to lend seriousness to the process and heighten team effort.

Seasonal Activities

Due to the nature of weight lifting, it is important to allow for body rest between workouts. This suggests alternate day scheduling if weight lifting is the only activity in the season. Another possibility is to do lower body lifting one day and upper body lifting the next. A third possibility is to incorporate other fitness activities, such as cardiovascular work, on alternate days. The particular example shown here used a Monday-Wednesday-Friday class schedule.

Each day, teams had designed workouts that specified exercises, number of sets, and number of repetitions to be performed (see Table 8.1). At the outset, teachers had to provide workout schedules, but as the season progressed captains and their teams designed workouts that met their specific needs. Weekly challenges were used as minicompetitions. These challenges typically focused on one of the lifts to be used in the final competition: incline press, bench press, squat, and clean.

Individual team members maintained personal record sheets of all workouts and lifts. Each lift has to be certified by a teammate to verify the accuracy of the weight and the legality of the lift. Individual team members turned in their records to captains. Captains maintained cumulative team records.

Early in the season, the focus was on correct technique, safety, and the benefits of strength training. As the season progressed, the focus shifted more to weekly competitions and preparation for final competition. The final competition was a team event in which total weight lifted across all events and weight divisions was the determining factor, thus emphasizing the team nature of the competition. Technique was also assessed, and awards were given to those who demonstrated good technique.

Student Roles

Students occupy roles as captains, judges, scorers, and publicists. The captain's role in a weight lifting season is crucial, not only for the

Table 8.1 Daily Team Workout Schedule

Day	Exercise	Sets	Reps
M,W,F	Clean	4	8–10
	Bench	6	8,8,6, 2,2,2
	Squat	6	8,8,6, 2,2,2
	Bent arm laterals	3	8–10
	Triceps push	3	8–10
	Toe raises	6	30

leadership in team development, but also because of safety implications. Safety is stressed early in the unit and continues to be stressed as correct lifting techniques are taught. The captain must be the safety leader for the team, not only as a model, but also ensuring that team members recognize and adhere to safety rules and procedures.

Captains also are responsible for supervising daily workouts of their teams early in the season when you prepare the workout schedule. As the season progresses, captains take a more active role with their teammates in designing workouts. Captains also prepare their teams for competitions and manage the team during the competitions.

Students are taught how to discriminate appropriate and inappropriate lifts and to certify weights. They practice these throughout the season because all new weight records require certification for them to count in individual and team performance records. Students also learn to judge competitions. Each team also can have a publicist who keeps bulletin boards and public records of performances up to date.

Performance Records and Awards

Individual and team performance records are kept, using a variety of categories: within each weight class, overall for each event, overall for each weight class, and overall team performance. These records provide the basis for end-of-season awards.

Team awards can also be used for each minicompetition and, of course, for the final team lifting event. The overall seasonal championship is typically determined by a combination of various performance records. Because technique is critical for effective strength development and necessary as a safety precaution, good technique awards also should be given to those who demonstrate such technique during competitions. As with most sport education applications, it also is appropriate to provide a special award for team captains who have fulfilled their responsibilities.

Student and Teacher Reactions

Students responded to a questionnaire regarding the sport education model. Student responses were extremely positive. They reported that the team format caused them to work harder and with more self-discipline than they do in a typical physical education class.

The teacher also was enthusiastic, having been convinced that more had been accomplished with more enthusiasm among students than in more traditional approaches. The teacher was particularly pleased with the performance progress of the class and attributed it to the motivation provided by the sport education format.

Running

In too many physical education programs, running is used as a punishment for tardiness or inappropriate behavior. Traditional fitness units also include running, but it is often done around a 400-meter (m) track and ends up being as much social walking as fitness-oriented running. Running can be the focus of a sport education season where different kinds of competitions maintain enthusiasm so that cardiovascular benefits can be maximized.

Sport and level: running, high school

Seasonal format: 20 to 25 lessons, daily or three times per week

Team format: teams selected through time trials

Competition formats: timed estimate run, power walking, handicap runs, orienteering, partner and team competitions

Student roles: captain, leader, scorekeeper, manager, trainer, race official

Performance records: individual training logs, team and individual competition performances, improvement records

Special features: awards, publicity, special events

Implementing the Running Season

Critical to the success of organizing fair teams is to conduct an initial series of time trials to rank students according to their current performance capacities. A variety of trials is useful because there will be a variety of training modes and competitions, such as 1-mile (1.6 m) handicap runs and 200-m pace challenges, emphasizing somewhat different running abilities. Using these rankings, captains and teams can be selected using any of the many methods described in this text.

Once teams are chosen, team members train and compete together throughout the season. Because a variety of running activities and competitions will be used, it helps to have team managers who organize teammates for competitions and keep team records. Coaches provide leadership in training and working with their teams. They also make decisions concerning competitions.

The key to a successful sport education running season is variety. A variety of activities allows students to recover from workouts and also provides a more psychologically stimulating season. Variety can be achieved in a number of ways.

- Changing the training site (track, park, wooded areas, etc.)
- Variety of training methods (Fartlek, power walking, intervals, pace work, long slow distance)
- Variety of intensities (hard or fast, moderate, easy or slow)
- Novel challenges (handicap events, orienteering, file runs)

Early in the season, the techniques of running and walking and necessary training for each competition provide the primary lesson focus. The season should be planned so that intensity and duration of workouts increases gradually. Special events like race walking and orienteering will need to be taught and practiced with frequent feedback to ensure appropriate technique.

Regular competitions should be planned because preparation for competition and team performance in competitions will become a primary motivating force throughout the season. Competitions, like workouts, should gradually increase in intensity, with different kinds of competitions interspersed throughout the season to allow for recovery. Some of the competitions that can be used are as follows.

Goal-Setting Challenges

Teams set individual and collective goals, monitor performance relative to those goals, and are awarded points for reaching the goals. Goals might include distances, times, adherence to workouts, and the like.

Timed Estimate Runs

Team members estimate the distance each can run in a set time or, conversely, the time it will take to run a set distance. Teams earn points for speed, distance covered, and accuracy of predictions.

Pace Workout Challenges

A set distance, number of repetitions, and recovery time are determined (for example, six repetitions of 200 m with 2-min recoveries). You can set different paces that reflect ability levels of students. The goal is for team members to stay within 3 seconds (s) (plus or minus) of their goal. Points are earned for each repetition that is within pace requirements.

Handicap Runs

Handicap runs should be used later in the season when fitness levels are improved and team members have clearly established their abilities. This allows you and coaches to establish accurate time handicaps for team members based on their performances. A specific distance—1 mile (1.6 km), 1.5 miles (2.4 km), 2 miles (3.2 km), etc.—is used. All runners run the same course. The clock begins when the slowest runners start the race. Each successive runner begins when their handicap time appears; for example, a runner with a 1.2-s handicap for the mile run will begin 1.2 s after the first runner. If handicaps are accurate, runners should finish bunched. Points are awarded based on place crossing the finish line.

Distance Running Challenges

This event can encourage out-of-class workouts. Teams determine a distance they want to run, which can be an out-of-class distance or it can incorporate both in-class and out-of-class workouts. Mileage is recorded on a workout-to-workout basis by the team manager as team members report distances. A motivating framework for distance running challenges the track team to progress by equating it with a run toward some particular place, such as from one city to another or across the state. Maps can be prepared and managers can track progress in reaching the destination.

Orienteering

Although orienteering is a sport in its own right that utilizes compass, map, and other equipment, it can be adapted for use in a running program. The teacher designs a course utilizing a variety of terrains and placing course markers at strategic points throughout the course. A map of the course with details on how to collect checkpoint tags is crucial to keeping all runners on the correct course. Runners can move at their own pace and collect points for teams based on performance. An alternative would be to have teams move through the course as units.

Student Roles, Records, and Awards

For a running season to progress smoothly, teams need to have captains, managers, and trainers. The captain's role is typical for sport education. Managers are responsible for keeping individual and team performance records up to date. They also help captains with entries for various competitions. Trainers become knowledgeable about various ailments and injuries associated with running. They can provide advice and guidance about stretching exercises.

Running is an activity where records can be kept for every workout and competition. Distances, times, paces, and time below or above goal times can be incorporated in records (see Table 8.2). To emphasize the team nature of the activity, post records in team rather than individual formats. Because improvement is a major goal, some performances should be posted based on improvement rather than on absolute times or distances.

Awards for the running season can be as diverse as the competitions themselves. Some awards can focus on workout records rather than competitions. Awards should recognize performance, improvement, and adherence to workout schedules.

Aerobics

Aerobic workouts have become part of the fitness landscape. Aerobic exercise usually is continuous and uses all major muscle groups; the intensity, duration, and frequency of exercise increase gradually. Most aerobic exercise is done to music, not only meeting workout criteria but also having potential aesthetic appeal. Aerobics in sport education can use a variety of formats, as you will read in this section.

Table 8.2 Timed Estimate Run 3-Mile Course

Name	Estimate	Actual time
Katie	21:10	
Mark	18:55	
David	19:20	
Jose	19:45	
Ladona	24:50	
Perry	25:00	
Geri	29:30	
Ed	23:30	
Nicole	27:15	

Sport and level: aerobics, high school

Seasonal format: 20 to 40 class sessions; daily, twice, or three times weekly

Team format: selected from rankings on cardiovascular trial

Competition formats: endurance competitions, routine development, heart rate competitions, strength and flexibility competitions

Student roles: performer, captain, designer, judge, fitness tester

Performance records: individual and team performance records, rankings or ratings in routine execution

Special features: shows, videotaping

Implementing the Aerobics Season

At the beginning of the season, measure the students for aerobic capacity—and for strength and flexibility if later competitions will focus on these fitness factors. You can choose from several aerobic fitness tests that have norms and allow for ranking students: the 12-min run-walk, the 1.5-mile run-walk, or the AAHPERD 1-mile run-walk. Another useful lesson to begin the season is teaching how to measure a pulse and having the students record their pulses at rest and at recovery.

After ranking the students by the appropriate fitness measures, form teams using any of the several methods described in this text. Captains should be chosen or elected primarily for leadership qualities, rather than fitness levels. Each team should have sufficient students to cover the range of fitness levels within the class. Teams should be large enough to perform aerobic routines as a group (at least six to eight students per team).

Teams should choose names quickly. They might also choose apparel, because colorful uniforms can add to the aesthetic appeal of routines. Teams should have home spaces in the gym and go to these spaces to begin the class.

If students meet daily, you might schedule a sport education session on Monday, Wednesday, and Friday with sport education aerobics on Tuesday and Thursday. Another possibility is scheduling sport education aerobics each day the physical education class meets. Sport education aerobics accommodates even a daily workout because a combination of high- and low-impact sessions allows students to recover sufficiently.

Early in the season the focus is on appropriate aerobic principles of warm-up, muscle groups, and progressive overload (frequency, duration, intensity). Students should learn the differences among high-impact aerobics, low-impact aerobics, step aerobics, and water aerobics. Flexibility and strength work should be differentiated from cardiovascular work. Students should learn early on how to measure heart rates accurately and quickly. At the same time, they should learn the concepts of resting heart rate, threshold-level heart rate, and recovery heart rate.

Schedule competitions frequently with a range of emphases: that is, endurance, technique, and aesthetic appeal. Explain how to judge aerobic routines. The kinds of competitions that can be used in sport education aerobics are as follows.

Endurance Competitions

Team and class challenges are appropriate. For example, schedule a high-impact aerobic session of 15 min where team members earn points by doing the exercises correctly and without break. Allow students who do the routine inappropriately or who need rest to take a 1-min time-out resuming the event afterward.

Routine Competitions

Teams should create routines to music they choose. The routines should develop according to specific criteria, such as equal attention to major muscle groups. Adherence to those exercise criteria, as well as the aesthetic appeal, forms the basis for judging the routine. Students from other teams should be judges.

Heart-Rate Competitions

Team competitions can focus on improving the heart rate (decrease in resting heart rate, for example), working continuously within a target range of heart rate, or recovery heart rate (after a set recovery time following a workout, students measure their heart rates to determine if they meet set criteria).

Strength and Flexibility Competitions

If you want to include strength and flexibility in the aerobics season, then competitions based on the several ways of measuring these fitness components can easily be arranged. Here too, a focus on improvement is as important as absolute measures.

Student Roles, Records, and Awards

The captain's role in aerobics is similar to other sport education applications, but in the aerobics application, leadership and motivation are particularly important qualities. Students can also occupy roles as routine-developers, judges, and exercise testers. Several team members might share the major responsibility of developing aerobic routines for their team. Other team members might represent the team as judges in routine competitions. Still other team members might be trained as exercise testers, taking the lead on their teams for the various measurements necessary to record performances based on cardiovascular, strength, or flexibility measures.

As with the running application, it is important that regular performance measures, such as resting and recovery heart rates, be kept by each student. These can be utilized in a team format as well as for individuals. A fair rating system should be developed for judging team performance in routines, and the system then can become part of the performance record. Again, as with running, awards should be based on both performance and improvement.

CHAPTER
9

Sport Education in the Secondary Curriculum

Donna Dugas
Nicholls State University

Secondary physical education programs typically have multiple programmatic and curricular goals. Quite frequently, lifetime sport participation and physical fitness are among the most prominent. In this chapter I describe how sport education can be incorporated in a total secondary program, especially to achieve the goals associated with sport participation. The examples used in the chapter are drawn from the program I directed at the Louisiana School for Math, Science and the Arts (LSMSA).

The total physical education program at LSMSA had three main organizing centers: leisure, fitness, and sport education. Class offerings within these three areas are listed in Table 9.1. These organizing centers are derived from statements of philosophy and goals that stress knowledge, skills, and attitudes. Students began the program with a required fitness course, after which they chose from among electives in the three organizing centers.

Table 9.1   Courses Offered in Three Program Areas

Sport education	Leisure	Fitness
Racquet sports	Recreational boating	Weight training
Badminton	Canoeing	Aerobic dance
Racquetball	Sailing	Aerobic exercises
Table tennis	Water skiing	
Tennis	Windsurfing	

(continued)

Table 9.1   *(continued)*

Sport education	Leisure	Fitness

Target Sports
  Archery
  Bowling
  Golf
  Fencing
  Riflery
Team sports
  Volleyball
  Track and field
  Flag football
  Basketball
  Baseball
  Softball
  Cross country
  Swimming
  Soccer
Martial arts
  Karate
	Aquatics
	  Beginning swimming
	  Intermediate swimming
	  Advanced lifesaving
	Recreational dance
	  Square and folk dances
	Additional offering
	  Backpacking and hiking	

Sports and level: 9 team sports and 14 individual sports in an elective program; high school

Seasonal format: school year divided into four nine-week seasons

Team format: teams chosen by students according to particular sport needs and class size

Competition formats: round-robins, ladders, dual meets, and so forth

Student roles: performer, captain, referee, scorekeeper, statistician, publicity, governing board

Performance records: statistics from performance in contests, written tests, officiating, score keeping

Special features: newspaper articles, bulletin boards, awards, sports newsletter

Curricular Format and Choice of Sports

Dividing the school year into four seasons fulfilled the sport education format of longer seasons and coincided with our four 9-week grading periods. In keeping with the sport education theme, we called the seasons fall, early winter, late winter, and spring (see Table 9.2). As much as possible, we scheduled sports for the season in which they occur in the larger sport culture: that is, touch football in the early fall, basketball in the winter, and softball in the spring. We also tried to offer a variety of individual and team sports, at least to the extent allowed by staffing constraints.

Other possibilities for scheduling sport education would be three 6-week seasons per semester with a total of six seasons for the school year. Another alternative would be to use a semester system with one sport education season per semester, allowing for an 18-week focus on a single sport.

Selection of Teams and Captains

Teams were formed at the outset of each season. In some cases, captains were selected by the teacher and then helped to select teams (see pages 22-24 for various selection procedures). In other cases, teams were formed

Table 9.2   Seasonal Schedule for Sport Education

Semester	Seasons	Team sports	Individual sports
Fall	Fall 9 weeks	Flag football Cross country	Tennis Archery Table tennis
Fall	Early winter 9 weeks	Volleyball Soccer	Fencing Bowling Badminton Racquetball
Spring	Late winter 9 weeks	Basketball Swimming	Fencing Bowling Racquetball Riflery
Spring	Spring 9 weeks	Baseball Softball Track and field	Badminton Golf Archery

through teacher-student discussion, and captains were elected by newly formed teams. In each case, the major goal was to create balance among teams to ensure fair competition. The total number of students who had elected that sport determined the number of teams and team size and the nature of competition.

Class Procedures and Instruction

Teachers agreed to develop course syllabuses in common so that each course format would protect the main features of sport education and hold students accountable in similar ways. Despite the fact that we used the term *coaches* instead of *teachers* and talked about seasons instead of units, we operated in an academic setting where grades are given for physical education and certain expectations for course materials prevail.

All sport education elective courses used a common format for course requirements and grading (see Table 9.3). The skill and strategy requirement is written based on league play; in other words, the student's ability to play skillfully and strategically during competition forms the basis for grading this requirement. The grade for skill and strategy is based on teacher evaluation of student performance during contests and also on the statistics compiled by student statisticians throughout the competitions. Refereeing and score keeping are also graded to add seriousness to these important sport education roles. The actual number of contests that students must participate in, referee, and score varies according to the sport, class size, and type of competition format being used.

The evaluation is based on a task-completion format. Even the written exam follows this format, with an 80-percent accuracy rate needed for task completion. I have found that a task-completion format results in a form of student-directed quality control. If students have tasks as officials, scorekeepers, and referees, for example, it is student feedback that results in quality performance. If student scorekeepers do not accomplish the task well, they will be quick to find out as student peers ask about their scores. The teacher needs to be a careful intervener in these situations, making sure that the quality-control feedback that students provide one another is appropriate and not spitefully presented. This whole system is a great opportunity for students to learn appropriate methods of interaction with one another. It is peer teaching and cooperative learning at its best. It also represents sport as it will be experienced in nonschool settings.

Student Roles

All sport education courses were designed to educate students as performers, officials, scorers, and managers. In addition, they have a clear

Table 9.3   Common Format for Course Requirements

Course requirements

1. A written exam on rules and regulations
2. Demonstration of skills and strategies during league play
3. Officiate league games
4. Keep official scorebook for league games
5. Participate in at least one optional activity
    a. Governing board
    b. Student coach
    c. Publicity
    d. Record keeping

Course evaluation

Written exam (50 points)	50
League play (8 at 15 points each)	120
Officiating (4 at 10 points each)	40
Scoring (4 at 5 points each)	20
Optional activity (20 points)	20
Total Points:	250

Course grade will be determined by the percentage of total points earned by the student.

    A 90–100% (225-250 points)
    B 80–89% (200-224 points)
    C 70–79% (175-199 points)
    D Below 70% (below 175 points)

focus on strategies, rules, and the history and rituals associated with various sports. This provided program continuity as students switched from one sport to another, often with different teachers: the purposes, format, and accountability systems remained consistent.

Course objectives included all the roles students would fill during the sport education season. Objectives were defined not only in terms of skill, strategy, and knowledge of rules, but also in terms of demonstrated skill in officiating and scoring, as well as participation in one optional activity. Optional activities for sport education seasons included (a) being a student coach, (b) participating as a member of the governing board, (c) participating on the record keeping committee, or (d) taking part in publicity committee work. When teams were chosen, by whatever system, team members had to decide which optional activity they would choose and make sure that all optional activities were covered within the team. It was through this optional-activity feature that most managerial work of a sport education season was done by students and that the real self-directed feature of sport education was played out.

The administrative work of each sport season is accomplished by students through their choice of optional activities. Students on the governing board assist in rule modifications, discipline for infractions, team selections, game preparations, and setting rules to ensure equitable playing time for all students. Students may be selected to the governing board by the teacher, but it is in keeping with the purposes of sport education that they be elected by students as soon as they understand the model.

Student coaches are responsible for conducting team practices with the assistance of the teacher, identifying starting lineups, coordinating equitable playing time, and alerting the teacher to potential problems within the team. Depending on the size of the class or the nature of the sport, teams often have cocaptains to share the many tasks related to the role. Student coaches should be selected by the class or by their teams based on clear criteria related to leadership and fairness. In mixed classes, it is a good idea to have cocaptains of both genders.

Some students choose publicity for their optional activity. These students become sports reporters. They are given a format to follow and they write their observations about games and use the scores and statistics in their stories. Their articles are submitted to the school or local newspapers. Students also videotape games and edit them as short news clips for local television and to replay for the class.

Record keeping is also an optional activity. Record keepers are also statisticians. The statistics recorded and publicized depend on the sport but both individual and team statistics can be kept. Record keepers are responsible for compiling and posting up-to-date statistics for their leagues and competitions. Examples are league standings, points for, points against, average points, and the like. Student coaches are encouraged to use information on their team's performance to plan strategy and practices.

Competitions

A number of different competition formats were used. Team sports, such as volleyball, soccer, and basketball, tended to be organized as leagues with round-robin formats. Since sport education emphasizes affiliation on a team as a major feature, even the individual sports, such as archery and golf, were organized on a team competition format.

In some sports, such as track and field and swimming, a series of meets were arranged, in which individual performance led to team points from which competitions were decided.

The number of students in any particular class and the gender balance of those students were determining factors in how the competitions were arranged. For example, with tennis and badminton competitions boys' and girls' singles, boys' and girls' doubles, and mixed doubles were used if the class size and gender balance allowed. In sports where gender is of no consequence, such as riflery and archery, teams competed without regard to gender.

Team Points and Awards

We tried to have many awards, but students were also working for grades in a school where grades are important. Each competition had an award system traditional for the sport. The major award was for the overall winner of seasonal competition. In some sports competition was organized by skill level, allowing for more awards: for example, in tennis, where awards were given for first singles, second singles, first doubles, and the like.

Publicists from each team kept track of the standings for each competition. These records were kept up-to-date, posted conspicuously in the gymnasium, and were publicized in the school newspaper. Keeping accurate performance records allowed for recognizing improvement, such as most improved 50-m freestyle performance or top defensive rebounder. Awards were presented after each season's culminating event.

The Impact of Sport Education

The impact of incorporating sport education into high school physical education was tremendous. Sport education allowed more students to succeed because it increased opportunities for success and redefined what it means to learn sport. Students reported positive reactions to their participation and it quickly became clear that they had more positive feelings toward the sports themselves, due no doubt to the success they found in the tasks they had to do responsibly in different roles for the sport education season to move forward smoothly.

I am convinced that discipline problems were reduced substantially. Students had more responsibility and in accepting those responsibilities tended to forego the inappropriate behaviors, the typical fooling around, that one sees so often in high school physical education classes. Lastly, sport education helped to develop better sportspersons: not only more skilled competitors and knowledgeable gamesplayers, but also young people who play fairly, appreciate the competitions, and acknowledge and respect the efforts of both teammates and opponents. It works!

In Part III we will explain how to evaluate students in an authentic manner through sport education, and we will also explore how the model might be extended to focus on the goals of Olympism as an educational movement.

PART
III

Evaluating and Broadening Student Experience

Part II gave you a good idea of the various ways in which sport education can be implemented, both for children at the elementary level and for youth at the secondary level. Now it's time to think about ways of evaluating student performance and about the possibility of extending the sport education model to make it even more meaningful and educationally relevant to students in today's world.

Chapter 10 describes how authentic assessment can be accomplished through the sport education model. Actually, authentic assessment is embedded in the sport education model through the production and utilization of related performance records. This form of assessment is truly authentic whereas skill testing, which we have grown accustomed to in physical education, is not. Assessment can sometimes be a time-consuming and not very satisfying chore for teachers, but in sport education that need not be. Students should learn how to observe performance and keep performance related statistics. These records can and should be used for assessment. They can be compiled and kept up to date by students as part of their sport education experience, thus freeing the teacher from the need to be a pencil pusher and record keeper all the time.

Chapter 11 extends sport education to incorporate global and multicultural education and personal development, which are the goals of Olympism, and which in turn provide a theme for sport education. That theme is the goals, symbols, and pageantry associated with Olympism and the Olympic Games. This chapter is of special interest to those of you who are dreamers and who look constantly for ways of presenting important educational goals to children and youth that capture their imagination and excite them. The Olympic curriculum can do just that!

10

Authentic Assessment Through Sport Education

Daryl Siedentop

The Ohio State University

Most physical education teachers have responsibilities for assessment and grading. Grading periods often mark important divisions of the school year. Physical education grades are compiled and reported differently from school to school. Some physical education teachers grade on attendance, dress, and participation without formal evaluation of learning outcomes. In many schools, students receive a physical education grade that reflects how well students behave in class rather than how skilled or fit they are or how much they improve. Some physical educators use skill tests and fitness tests as objective measures for assessment and grading purposes. When physical education teachers gather to discuss school issues, few topics are more controversial than assessment and grading practices.

The most common forms of evaluation in physical education are end-of-unit assessments. Sometimes these are skill tests or written tests. Sometimes they are global, subjective evaluations by teachers. Except for attendance lists and dress cuts little effort is made to produce a regular strategy of assessment throughout a unit. When students get a grade in physical education, it is often hard for them to know what contributed to the grade or how the judgments about it were made. Sport education, on the other hand, provides a means for making assessment regular and much more authentic than is typical.

Authentic Assessment

Over the past 10 years a movement has gained momentum to make assessment and grading more authentic. This movement toward alternative systems of assessment stems from the notion that assessment should relate directly to outcomes that are important and relevant. In assessing how well students write, for example, the authentic assessment movement stresses writing essays and stories, rather than completing multiple choice tests about writing. Authentic assessment has been done for years in some segments of physical education. For example, in a swimming class where the goal is to use the crawl stroke for one lap of the pool, the assessment is simply to swim one lap of the pool using the crawl stroke. That is an important and relevant outcome because swimming one lap independently clearly reflects the ability to swim similar distances on different occasions.

Other forms of assessment in physical education are less authentic, particularly those associated with skill tests. Think, for example, of a wall-rally in tennis as a skill test for the forehand stroke. This kind of test is often used as an assessment for grading purposes in a tennis unit. The goal is to learn to play tennis, but rallying a tennis ball off a wall is not an authentic indicator of how well you play the game. Think, also, of a volleyball skill test where one student lobs a ball to a partner who executes a forearm pass. Is this like the skill that student will need when playing in a game and attempting to execute the forearm pass, for example when returning a serve? No, it is clearly unlike game play.

Most skill testing is time consuming and is marginally related to main learning goals. Skill testing, however, produces numbers, scores that can be used as objective measures of skill development. A skill test *score* is objective, but the *skill* has little relevance. Sport education, on the other hand, provides for a more authentic form of assessment as part of the basic model's implementation.

Assessment in Sport Education

The chapters in this text provide numerous examples of authentic assessment, all done as regular parts of the sport education season. Nearly every sport education model described includes examples of assessment of student performance that is authentically related to class goals and can, if desired, be used for evaluation and grading purposes.

• In the elementary gymnastics model, students use skill checklists to determine their level of competition. These checklists could also be used for assessment purposes. The checklists show progress and successful completion of relevant gymnastics skills.

• In the elementary gymnastics model, student execution of routines in competition are evaluated by the teacher, but the evaluation could also be used for assessment purposes. The routine is a series of skills linked together to produce an overall aesthetic effect. It is the kind of performance that is relevant in the world of gymnastics, and it represents an authentic performance goal for gymnastics education.

• In several models, written tests about playing and refereeing the sport are used.

• In the middle school volleyball model, students do a skill hustle every day, with captains recording performances. These daily performances are compiled and presented as seasonal performances. They also provide useful assessment information. These records show both improvement over the course of the season and absolute performance levels.

• In the high school strength model, there are daily and weekly challenges as well as performance records for lifting throughout the season. What better assessment data could a teacher use for evaluation purposes? These records could be used to determine improvement as well as absolute performance levels.

• In the high school curriculum model, course objectives for the sport education season are presented along with an evaluation of those objectives. The data for these evaluations are compiled as a regular part of student work during the sport education season.

Assessment Systems in Sport Education

Teachers at the elementary level favor seasonal point systems as a method of determining awards for sport education. Two features of these point systems are noteworthy in terms of their application to assessment and evaluation. First, actual data collection for points is typically done by students. For example, captains report their teams' attendance and dress for each class session. Student performance in contests is recorded by student scorekeepers and reported to the teacher. This feature relieves teachers of spending most of their time on assessment activities.

A second feature worthy of note is that nearly any activity that a teacher believes is valuable for assessment could be included in an overall point system. In the systems described in elementary models, teachers give points for teams being on task for the lesson, teams doing warm-ups appropriately, teams practicing at recess, and the like. It is clear from those chapters that teachers of young children believe that social objectives such as cooperation, fair play, and staying on task are important ingredients in a successful elementary physical education program. The sport education model provides a system for assessing and reporting performance that relates to these objectives.

With older students, the methods for assessment and the kinds of data used can be more sophisticated. The secondary model shown in chapter 9 specifies course objectives and course evaluation based on those objectives. A key feature of this assessment model is that all relevant sport education goals are included in the assessment strategy. Students are evaluated when they referee and keep score, but the performance counts less toward the overall grade than do demonstrations of skill and strategy in contests (see page 109). Of course, the information used in judging skill and strategy performance comes from data compiled by students during the competition season. The contest-by-contest data are accumulated by other students as part of their duties in the optional activities (see page 110). These same data are used by the teacher to assess the performance aspects of the grade. Students take these data collection and accumulation chores seriously for two reasons. First, performance in these duties is part of the grade. Second, and perhaps more importantly, there is built-in accountability from their peers because players on all teams want to know how they are doing individually and how their teams are doing collectively. Thus, they want accurate records and they want them up to date.

What is clear is that the teachers have produced systems that incorporate what they value in the goals of the sport education model. Each system operates a bit differently, but they share such common features as students acting as data collectors and reporters, social goals, such as fair play and cooperative behavior, and regular measurement of performance rather than end-of-unit global judgments or skill tests.

Sport education, therefore, incorporates the means for providing authentic assessment for children and youth in PE. Nothing special need be done, other than to implement the model. Students learn to observe and record performance as part of what they learn in sport education. These data can be used for several purposes, but they are clearly important for assessment.

The next chapter will show how the sport education model can be extended to incorporate the noble educational goals associated with Olympism and become a vehicle through which multicultural and global education can be emphasized.

11

Extending Sport Education: The Olympic Curriculum

Daryl Siedentop

The Ohio State University

Schools are changing in response to the demands of a new economic and political world. Physical education must also change if it is to occupy a valued place in the curriculum of twenty-first century schools. For a physical education curriculum to be successful it must capture the imagination of both teachers and students. It must also contribute to major educational goals. Certainly, it is now clear that several of these goals are a better understanding of the world, a better appreciation and respect for a multicultural world, the ability to be both a leader and a cooperative member of a working group, and the ability to persevere at tasks despite obstacles and setbacks. Fortunately for physical education, there is an educational movement, rooted in sport, that is designed to meet all these challenges and goals. That educational movement is Olympism.

Olympism provides an exciting and relevant concept on which to build a physical education curriculum that contributes to the full education of children and youth. The first principle of the Olympic Charter, which describes the purposes of the Olympic movement, is "to educate young people through sport in a spirit of better understanding between each other and of friendship, thereby helping to build a better and more peaceful world" (United States Olympic Committee Education Committee, p. 13). At no time in history is this educational goal more relevant than it is today, as we approach the twenty-first century in a world that has grown increasingly interdependent.

Olympism is also about making the words of the Olympic creed a real part of the lives of children and youth: "The most significant thing in the Olympic Games is not to win but to take part. Just as the most important thing in life is not the triumph but the struggle. The essential thing is not to have conquered but to have fought well" (p. 17). Taking part, overcoming obstacles, and striving to be the best you can be are qualities that many physical educators value. In Olympism they become the central focus of the educational program.

Olympism as the Organizing Concept for Sport Education

The sport education model described throughout this text has captured the enthusiasm of both teachers and students. The described variations of sport education show that the model can accommodate many different sports, fitness activities, grade levels, and school schedules. Sport education strives to bring out the best in sport and make it available to all students. This chapter describes how to extend the sport education model to use the aims and goals of Olympism to create an Olympic curriculum.

Most students and teachers are very much aware of the Olympic Games, which are perhaps the greatest sports festivals in history. Fewer are aware, however, of the educational movement called Olympism, the term used by Baron Pierre de Coubertin, the founder of the modern Olympic Games, to describe the plan of educational reform that he hoped would be sparked by the rejuvenation of the Olympic Games in 1896. From the outset, the concept of Olympism was an educational philosophy that sought to integrate academic study, aesthetic education, moral education, and physical education (Lucas, 1981). The catalyst for this integration was sport; thus, the sport education model is an appropriate vehicle through which to articulate a modern physical education curriculum based on the concept of Olympism.

As Osterhoudt (1981) has argued, Olympism is the movement through which education in sport reaches its fullest potential.

It [Olympism] embodies the illumination, the apotheosis, toward which all sport (and for that matter all human endeavor) authentically disposed tends. The basis of this contention stems from the unmatched, the intrinsic depth and nobility of inspiration that Olympism gains from an idea of human life at its compelling best. No movement having to do with sport has so fully connected itself to the foundations of human life per se as has Olympism; no movement having to do with sport has so fully captured the sense of such an ideal. Olympism has brought sport nearer its fully human possibilities than any other modern event. (p. 354)

The concept of Olympism has the power to attract the enthusiasm of teachers, and to provide a meaningful reason for them to invest themselves in the physical education of their students. Olympism also has the power to inspire children and youth to help them become the best they can be.

The Aims and Goals
of the Olympic Curriculum

This text demonstrates that the sport education model can successfully educate children and youth more completely in the areas of sport and fitness, and that it can do so in a way that fosters individual responsibility (through specific student roles) and the ability to work effectively within groups (through affiliation with teammates for the duration of a sport season). The Olympic curriculum is meant to extend this model so that the high values of the Olympic charter and the Olympic creed are made educationally relevant and meaningful in the lives of children and youth. To do so, the Olympic curriculum incorporates peace education, global education, multicultural education, and aesthetic education within the sport education model.

The Olympic curriculum incorporates peace education in the sense that it emphasizes moral and ethical behavior, particularly as they apply to sport, and focuses further on commitments to friendship and peace among individuals, groups, and nations. This is accomplished at the immediate level by a strong focus on personal control and the commitment to be both a strong individual and a productive member of cooperative groups. It is accomplished at an extended level by students who understand and become more predisposed to extend those qualities to relationships among racial, ethnic, and cultural groups and nations.

The Olympic curriculum incorporates global education by helping students become knowledgeable about the nations in the Olympic family and by stressing the need for cooperation among nations. It focuses on multicultural education by making students more knowledgeable about and respectful of the ethnic, religious, and racial differences in the Olympic family. It teaches tolerance and respect for diversity among the peoples of the world.

The aesthetic education component focuses on the beauty of sport, the aesthetics of the human body in motion, and the manner in which music, art, and literature can be related to and supportive of the purposes of Olympism. These various components are not meant to be mutually exclusive. Obviously, the art and music of a distant nation cannot only contribute to the aesthetic component of Olympism but can also help to achieve the multicultural and global education components.

The main goals of the Olympic curriculum are

• to develop competent, literate, and enthusiastic sport persons (see page 4 for a further explanation of these sport education goals);

• to develop self-responsibility and the ability to persevere in the pursuit of goals;

• to work effectively within a group toward common goals;

• to know and respect differences among cultures and ethnic and racial groups; to value diversity; to become predisposed to work toward a more peaceful world; and

• to know and respect the value and beauty of the human body in motion; the aesthetic value of working together in competition; and the manner in which art, music, and literature are related to and supportive of Olympism.

The Olympic curriculum might be used at any level, starting with the upper elementary grades, where the cognitive and moral development of students makes the goals immediately relevant. As with the sport education models shown in this text, the Olympic model could be used in a simplified version by one teacher. However, the curriculum would have its greatest impact as a central PE theme in a school where all teachers use the curriculum and contribute to achieving its goals. Adopted as a district-wide curriculum, the curriculum's impact would be even greater.

Underlying Structural Principles

Most of the structural principles for the Olympic curriculum are identical to those used in sport education. They are reviewed here briefly. The reader should consult chapters 1 and 2 for more thorough explanations of these principles.

• Longer units of instruction than typical in physical education, with units referred to as seasons

• Student membership on teams for the season's duration, creating an affiliation through which personal growth and group objectives can be attained

• A formal schedule of competition, creating choices for teams and incentives for improvement

• A culminating event to close the season, creating a festive conclusion that fulfills incentives and provides recognition

• Developing and maintaining a festive atmosphere in which taking part is valued and student success is noted and celebrated in many ways

- The recording and sharing of team and individual performance records

- Students becoming familiar with major roles associated with successful sport, such as referee, scorekeeper, coach, trainer, publicist, manager, and the like

In addition to these sport education principles, four additional structural principles are necessary to extend the sport education model to the Olympic curriculum.

- During each season, teams represent nations in the Olympic family, thus becoming "national" teams for the duration of the season.

- Some specific model for personal growth and working within a group should be adopted and integrated into the incentive and recognition system.

- Academic integration in social studies, art, music, and literature should be incorporated as time and resources permit.

- The festive component should be based on Olympic protocols.

A Standard Format
for the Olympic Curriculum

Different scheduling formats for physical education at different grade levels and in different districts require a flexible approach to delivering the Olympic curriculum. Experience with the sport education model suggests that widely different formats can be adopted to pursue basic curricular goals while preserving its main structural principles. What follows as a standard format could be adopted by individual teachers, physical education departments, or school districts.

- Organizing the school year. The school year should be divided into four or five seasons. Each season lasts from seven to nine weeks. The choice here is most often determined by the school schedule itself, especially when teachers are required to turn in grades for specific grading periods, because it is often efficient for teachers to align seasons with school grading periods. Season length allows for the accomplishment of the diverse goals of the Olympic curriculum.

- The "national" team as the affiliation format. As in sport education, students are members of teams, but in the Olympic curriculum each team represents a nation. Organizing students into teams can be done in any of the various ways described in chapter 2 and throughout the text. Once teams are organized, team members represent a nation in the Olympic family. Each team in the class should represent a nation in a different continent. If the three-team format so popular in sport education is utilized (see page 24), then three different continents should be represented (the symbol of the Olympic rings signifies the five continents comprising the Olympic family). Teams can choose nations from within those continents or they can be assigned by teachers. All of the competitions and records can, therefore, be organized by national teams. Once a nation has been chosen for a season by a team, it is appropriate to disallow that choice by another team for the remainder of the school year. If the Olympic curriculum is used throughout the physical education program, then it makes sense that the same nations should be represented by each class during the length of a particular season. This would allow for more continuity in using materials and would make the gymnasium a festive place. It would also allow for some interesting nonattached-time extensions. For example, if one of the nations for a soccer season is Zimbabwe, representing the continent of Africa, an intramural competition (a kind of national championship for Zimbabwe) might be arranged for all ninth-grade class teams who had represented Zimbabwe during the season.

• The Olympic committee.   Many teachers have chosen to include a sports committee or sports board as a feature in their sport education models (see page 25). This is a particularly beneficial feature in middle and secondary school because it provides a major role for students and creates a mechanism whereby decisions can be made and disputes arbitrated by students themselves, thus contributing to the personal-growth goals of the curriculum. The sports board would, in the Olympic curriculum, function as an Olympic committee.

• Choosing the sports.   Each season should focus on a different Olympic sport. Selection of sports is left to the individual teachers, schools, or districts. Sports should be selected that represent different combinations of strength, skill, strategy, and aesthetic qualities (see page 19). As in sport education, small-sided, modified sports are preferred, allowing for progressive skill and strategy development as well as more active participation by all students (see pages 20-21).

• Integrating academic work to meet the global, multicultural, and aesthetic education goals.   During the season in which students represent a national team, they learn about the country they represent as well as those represented by classmates. The feature allows for substantial integration with social studies, art, music, and literature. National colors and anthems can be used to add to the festive atmosphere. Music, art, and poetry from the various nations can be incorporated as appropriate. Much of this can be done as homework or integrated with the classroom teacher's work. Students can also learn about the national sports of each country and their major sport figures. Students might create their own Olympic awards as art projects.

- Formalizing the personal development goals of the curriculum. Olympism is dedicated to creating a more peaceful world; working together; friendly competition; and learning to strive to be the best that you can be. The personal and social development goals of Olympism are central to its overall purposes. It is clear that teachers who have used the sport education model have found that among its most important outcomes is the social development that derives from accepting and fulfilling responsible roles within a team structure. Thus, one might expect a substantial amount of personal and social development in the Olympic curriculum because it uses the same format. Teachers, however, might want to emphasize personal and social development goals even more by formalizing them. There are many ways to do this. Hellison's (1978, 1983, 1984) work on social development provides a multilevel model of increasing personal and social responsibility. Figure 11.1 shows an application of this model for elementary physical education. Table 11.1 shows an application for middle or secondary school.

A second approach would be to emphasize and formally develop a fair player system. Table 11.2 shows characteristics of fair and unfair players. Figure 11.2 shows a similar approach as developed by Fair Play Canada. Figure 11.3 shows yet another fair play model developed in New Zealand by the Hillary Commission for Sport Fitness and Leisure. The point of using any version of these systems is to clearly specify the positive behavioral characteristics that teachers want students to develop and show as well as those to be avoided. These characteristics can then be used in instruction, can lend specificity to feedback concerning these goals, and can also be used in the incentive and award system.

- Creating a festive Olympic atmosphere. The Olympic movement provides many symbols and rituals that can be easily incorporated into the Olympic curriculum to develop and sustain a festive atmosphere. Suggestions include using the Olympic rings and creed as large, permanent posters in the gym, using the athlete and referee oaths prior to the beginning of each season's competition, and playing the Olympic hymn prior to end of season award ceremonies. Teachers can also use materials from the countries represented by national teams to build and sustain a festive atmosphere. Suggestions include using national flags and national colors, having students develop bulletin boards providing information and pictures on their "home" countries, and using national anthems in ceremonies.

This standard format could be adapted to local needs, yet still maintain the underlying structural principles. Some schools might want to have more slightly shorter seasons. Some schools might want to keep students on teams for an entire semester or school year (see chapter 5). Some

What's Your Level?

Level 0: Irresponsibility

Home: blaming brothers or sisters for problems

Playground: calling other students names

Classroom: talking to friends when teacher is giving instructions

Physical education: pushing and shoving others when selecting equipment

Level 1: Self-control

Home: keeping self from hitting brother even though really mad at him

Playground: standing and watching others play

Classroom: waiting until appropriate time to talk with friends

Physical education: practicing but not all the time

Level 2: Involvement

Home: helping to clean up supper dishes

Playground: playing with others

Classroom: listening and doing class work

Physical education: trying new things without complaining and saying I can't

Level 3: Self-responsibility

Home: cleaning room without being asked

Playground: returning equipment during recess

Classroom: doing a science project not a part of any assignment

Physical education: undertaking to learn a new skill through resources outside the physical education class

Level 4: Caring

Home: helping take care of a pet or younger child

Playground: asking others (not just friends) to join in play

Classroom: helping another student with a math problem

Physical education: willingly working with anyone in the class

Figure 11.1   Hellison's levels for the elementary physical program.
Note. This figure is reprinted with permission from the **JOPERD** (Journal of Physical Education, Recreation and Dance), September, 1990, pp. 18-19. **JOPERD** is a publication of the American Alliance for Health, Physical Education, Recreation and Dance, 1900 Association Drive, Reston, VA 22091-1599.

Table 11.1   Hellison's Responsibility Levels as Used in Middle and High School Physical Education

Level zero: cut from the team
- Frequently absent or tardy
- Abuses others
- Interrupts practice

Level I: benched
- Absent or tardy several times
- Off task in practice but not abusive or disruptive

Level II: player
- Good attendance
- Is coachable and on task at practice
- Does not abuse others or interrupt practice

Level III: self-coach
- Good attendance
- Is coachable and on task at practice
- Does not abuse others or interrupt practice
- Is able to set personal goals and work independently on these goals

Level IV: coach
- Good attendance
- Is coachable and on task at practice
- Does not abuse others or interrupt practice
- Is able to set personal goals and work independently on these goals
- Possesses good helping skills: can give cues, observe and give specific positive feedback as well as general praise
- Encourages teamwork and passing the ball
- Listens to players; is sensitive to their feelings and needs
- Puts the welfare of players above own needs
- Understands that the key to being a good coach is not basketball ability, but rather the foregoing characteristics.

Note. From "Teaching Values Through Basketball" by D. Hellison and N. Georgiadis, 1992, *Strategies*, **5**(4), pp. 5-8. Copyright 1992 by D. Hellison & N. Georgiadis. Reprinted by permission.

teachers might want to emphasize personal growth in the curriculum and downplay the aesthetics or global education. Some teachers will find it difficult to integrate art, music, and literature as fully as they desire. None of these restrictions or differences in outlook need detract from pursuing the main goals of the Olympic curriculum.

It is also advisable for teachers to begin the Olympic curriculum effort with a basic model, implement it well, and then add to it as students become accustomed to the model and teachers have more time to devote to generating resources for developing the model more fully. For example, when students have projects to develop information about

Table 11.2   Fair Player and Unfair Player Characteristics

Fair player characteristics	Unfair player characteristics
-Follows rules	-Criticizes play of others
-Accepts officials' calls	-Yells at officials
-Compliments good play of others	-Blames mistakes on others
-Encourages teammates	-Bosses other players
-Plays own position	-Hogs space and dominates play
-Helps less-skilled classmates	-Makes fun of those less skilled
-Is gracious in victory and defeat	-Gloats in victory, sulks in defeat
-Tries hard to apply skills	-Won't work unless at center of
-Plays under control	play
-Wants everybody to play and	-Loses temper frequently
succeed	-Favors only a few classmates
-Plays hard but fair	-Tries to use rules to gain advantage

Note. From *Fair Play in the Gym: Race and Sex Equity in Physical Education* (pp. 132-133) by P. Griffin and J. Placek, 1983, Amherst: University of Massachusetts, Women's Equity Program. Copyright 1983 by Pat Griffin. Adapted by permission.

the nation they represent, the materials from these projects can be used in later years, thus building a backlog of Olympic curriculum resources. Also, as teachers in the school learn about the Olympic curriculum, they will see ways they can contribute to it through student work and projects in various classes, especially in art, music, and literature, but also in social studies.

Incentive, Evaluation, and Award System

The incentive, evaluation, and award systems in the Olympic curriculum can be fully integrated. Incentives provide motivation to work toward goals. Student performance becomes the data for assessment of progress, a more authentic form of assessment than is typically available (see chapter 10). Awards are given for progress and accomplishment based on those assessments.

The traditional award system of the Olympics—gold, silver, and bronze—can be used effectively in the Olympic curriculum. In most cases, however, the achievement of any specific award should be based on meeting task-related criteria rather than competing with others. The goal should always be for as many students as possible to meet specified criteria and thus earn gold medals. The many kinds of awards described throughout this text—captain's awards, fair play awards, most improved awards,

Fair Play Agreement

For the Player	For the Teacher
I _____	I _____
Agree to:	Agree to:
• always play by the rules	• remember that students play for fun
• never argue with an official	• encourage my students and offer constructive criticism
• remember that I am playing because I enjoy the sport	• instruct my students to follow both the letter and the spirit of the rules
• work at achieving my personal best	
• show appreciation for good plays and good players	• teach students that officials are important parts of the game
• control my temper and not be a show-off	• encourage my students to be good sports
• play fairly at all times	• give every participant a chance to play and to learn the skills
_____ signature	• remember that my actions speak louder than my words
	_____ signature

Date _____

Figure 11.2 A fair play agreement.
Note. From "Fair Play—It's Your Call!: A Resource Manual for Coaches" (p. 25) by Fair Play Canada. Copyright 1993 by Fair Play Canada. Adapted by permission.

extra practice awards, and the like—can be conceptualized as gold, silver, and bronze, each representing a higher level of improvement or accomplishment. The gold-silver-bronze format also lends itself well to the formal competition aspects of the curriculum because so many teachers have had success using the three-team-per-class format, ensuring that each team wins an award for overall competitive success.

Personal development goals should be incorporated into the award system. This suggests that a three-level model would allow for bronze, silver, and gold medal levels for personal and social development.

Many teachers have incorporated additional student roles into sport education to involve students in tasks that are related to the smooth and effective completion of a season, such as publicist, statistician, and the like. It would be quite easy to have one or two members of each team in the class serve on an awards committee and create gold, silver, and bronze awards for the various major aspects of the incentive award system. These awards might range from captain's certificates to gold,

Without Fair Play Sport Is No Longer Sport

Fair play is a way of behaving. It involves

- honesty;
- respect for teammates;
- respect for opponents, whether winning or losing; and
- respect for referees and umpires.

Player's Code

- Play for the "fun of it" and not just to please teachers or parents.
- Play by the rules.
- Never argue with officials.
- Control your temper.
- Be a good sport.
- Treat all players as you would like to be treated.
- Cooperate with your teacher, teammates, and opponents. Without them there would be no game.

Figure 11.3   Fair play guidelines.
Note. From various publications from Hillary Commission for Sport, Fitness and Leisure, Wellington, New Zealand. Adapted by permission.

silver, and bronze fair play pins, to actual medals. It is important to note that the length of the season is crucial to making these kinds of outside-of-class tasks meaningful and justifiable.

Using Olympic Protocols to Create a Festive Atmosphere

A fundamental principle of sport education is the creation and maintenance of a festive atmosphere, celebrating progress, accomplishment, and the joy of involvement in sport. Teachers who have used sport education have found many exciting ways to maintain a festival atmosphere—bulletin boards, posters, sport newsletters, columns in school papers, hallway displays, team colors, formal ceremonies at culminating events, and the like.

In the Olympic curriculum, it makes sense to utilize Olympic protocols as much as possible. The symbols of the Olympic movement have been chosen carefully to project the goals of Olympism. The rings representing the continents on the Olympic flag are interlocked, symbolizing the union of the five continents and the meeting of athletes throughout the world in the spirit of fair play and friendly competition. Doves, representing peace, are a part of the opening Olympic ceremonies. The enduring flame of the Olympic torch symbolizes the lasting nature of that peace.

The main Olympic symbols—the name, emblems, and terminology—are protected under the Amateur Sports Act of 1978. The United States Olympic Committee (USOC) has the exclusive right to use or authorize the use of the names and symbols of the Olympic movement. The USOC, however, has authorized the use of these Olympic symbols for educational purposes by nonprofit or educational institutions, provided they are used for the purpose of increasing awareness and understanding of Olympic ideals and Olympism (United States Olympic Committee Education Committee, n.d., p. 15). Since this is the purpose of the Olympic curriculum described in this chapter, it is clear that teachers can use the symbols and ideas of the Olympic movement in their educational endeavors.

Some specific suggestions for using Olympic symbols and terminology to create and maintain a festive atmosphere throughout the Olympic curriculum are as follows.

• Create a large Olympic flag and display it in a prominent place in the gymnasium, referring to it often for the symbolism it displays.

• Create a large poster displaying the Olympic creed for a high spot on a main wall in the gymnasium. "The most significant thing in the Olympic Games is not to win but to take part. Just as the most important thing in life is not the triumph but the struggle. The essential thing is not to have conquered but to have fought well" (United States Olympic Committee Education Committee, p. 17). Use it frequently for related instruction and feedback. Constantly tie it into the personal and social development program of the curriculum.

• At the beginning of formal competition for each season, have one athlete say the Olympic oath on behalf of all competitors in the class. Have another student say the official's oath on behalf of all students.

• Prominently display the characteristics of personal and social development that you have chosen to formalize those goals, such as levels of responsibility, fair and unfair player characteristics, and fair play contracts.

• Prior to culminating events, have a procession of athletes representing nations using the national anthem of each nation.

• For the length of the season when a nation is represented, display the flag of that nation, perhaps on a bulletin board with other information.

• At the culminating awards ceremony play the Olympic anthem as awards are being made, signifying that competitions are among teams and players, rather than among nations.

A readily available resource about Olympics and Olympism issues is *Olympic Day in the Schools*, materials that the United States Olympic Committee's Education Committee publishes.

Epilogue

We have written this book to be practical. Teachers lead busy lives, dominated by concerns about the next few minutes, the next lesson, the next day. Much is being written about the need for teachers to be more reflective, but the free time that reflection requires is all too limited. Still, in some spare moment, it is important that physical educators reflect about sport and its potential.

Although this book has presented a model to teach sport in physical education, it has also implicitly addressed the role of sport in modern societies. We allotted little space to explaining why sport warrants a curricular focus. Nor could we review why noted intellectuals and academics like Michael Novak, Paul Weiss, and A. Bartlett Giamatti have focused their substantial talents to serious works about the importance of sport in individual lives and in culture.

Our apparent lack of attention to the philosophical issues of sport does not mean we think them unimportant. Sport is central to our culture; evidence of its importance abounds. Sport has the power to influence children and youth, for good and for bad.

In *Take Time for Paradise: Americans and Their Games*, Bart Giamatti (1989), former president of Yale University and the late commissioner of baseball, argues that sport is an expression of human freedom. His rationale would find considerable support in the academic literature.

So games, contests, sports reiterate the purpose of freedom every time they are enacted—the purpose being to show how to be free and to be complete and connected, unimpeded, and integrated, all at once. The very elaborations of sport—its internal conventions of all kinds, its ceremonies, its endless meshes entangling itself—are for the purpose of training and testing and rewarding the rousing motion within us to find a moment of freedom. Freedom is that state where energy and order merge and all complexity is purified into a simple coherence, a fitness of parts and purpose and passions that cannot be surpassed and whose goal could only be to be itself. (p. 104)

Such beautiful language and lofty ideals may seem far removed from helping fifth or seventh graders learn to do and to value volleyball, tennis, or gymnastics. But the connection between those educational experiences and the opportunity to participate in that "state where energy and order merge and all complexity is purified into a simple coherence" is in large part what sport education is all about.

Perhaps this important connection is easier to see in the writing of *New York Times* columnist Anna Quindlen (1992), who in the summer of the 1992 Olympic Games nostalgically examined her feelings on the occasion of her 40th birthday. Looking back at her sport experience as a girl, she remarked that her only regret was not being a member of the "dream team."

> Catholic schoolgirls once played intramural basketball all winter long, and though it was with a smaller ball and slacker rules than the boys used—and though I traveled more often than I ever scored— it gave me a visceral feeling for the nonpareil grace, skill and team- work of the sport. Not to mention that glow in your chest when the ball leaves your hands, arcs through the air with all eyes following, and falls almost inevitably through the hoop. Yessss . . . There's a moment when the ball arcs perfectly downward to the waiting web of the net—or when the words lie down just right on the page—that makes you feel as if you could live forever.

Of course, we can't live forever, so any experience that gives us the feeling that we can should be cherished and protected. But the same experiences that carry so much positive potential always seem to have the potential for corruption as well. Here, too, in this distinction be- tween positive and negative outcomes in sport, one can see the underly- ing purposes of sport education. We began this book by suggesting that sport education seeks to preserve, protect, and enhance the cultures of sport so that more people may have more opportunities to experience freedom in ways that are uncorrupted by negative influences.

So despite the practical, nontheoretical nature of this book, deeply important issues are at stake. Be assured that your day-to-day efforts to educate children and youth in sport have a larger goal both in students' lives and in the larger, collective life of our society.

"Sport for all" is a noble goal, but at the moment it is unrealized. Race, gender, socioeconomic status, and skill level are still barriers that prevent us from achieving a sane, participatory sport culture. School physical education is still the only process that has the potential for reaching all children and youth, to educate them toward an appro- priate and personally satisfying lifelong sport involvement. If education in sport is left to others inevitably sport programs will be less available to children and youth based on gender, race, socioeconomic status, and skill level. If we believe that sport has the power to provide meaningful moments and valuable experiences, then we need to ensure that educa- tion in sport is fair and appropriate. In a sense, we have to guarantee that the field of opportunity to learn and enjoy sport is a level playing field for all children and youth.

References

Canadian Commission for Fair Play. (n.d.). *Fair play for kids*. Minister of State for Fitness and Amateur Sport, Government of Canada.

Giamatti, A.B. (1989). *Take time for paradise: Americans and their games*. New York: Summit Books.

Grant, B. (1992). Integrating sport into the physical education curriculum in New Zealand secondary schools. *Quest*, **44**(3), 304-316.

Griffin, P., & Placek, J. (1983). *Fair play in the gym: Race and sex equity in physical education*. Amherst: University of Massachusetts, Women's Equity Program.

Hellison, D. (1978). *Beyond balls and bats: Alienated youth in the gym*. Washington, DC: American Alliance for Health, Physical Education, Recreation and Dance.

Hellison, D. (1983). Teaching self responsibility (and more). *Journal of Physical Education, Recreation and Dance*. **54**(7), 23.

Hellison, D. (1984). *Goals and strategies for teaching physical education*. Champaign, IL: Human Kinetics.

Hellison, D., & Georgiadis, N. (1992). Teaching values through basketball. *Strategies*. **5**(4), 5-8.

Hillary Commission for Recreation and Sport. (n.d.). *Fair play sport*. Wellington, New Zealand.

Lucas, J. (1981). The genesis of the modern Olympic Games. In J. Seagrave & D. Chu, *Olympism* (pp. 22-32). Champaign, IL: Human Kinetics.

Masser, L. (1990). Teaching for affective learning in elementary physical education. *Journal of Physical Education, Recreation and Dance*. **62**(7), 18-19.

Osterhoudt, R. (1981). Modern Olympism in the conjunction of nineteenth and twentieth century civilization: Olympism as the transformative concept of purpose and the human in modern sport. In J. Seagrave & D. Chu. *Olympism* (pp. 347-362). Champaign, IL: Human Kinetics.

Quindlen, A. (1992, July 12). Feeling fully 40, ex-ballplayer exults in Dream Team's excellence. *Columbus Dispatch*, p. 3H.

Siedentop, D. (1981, August). Must competition be a zero-sum game? *The School Administrator*, **38**, 11.

Siedentop, D. (1987). The theory and practice of sport education. In G. Barrette, R. Feingold, R. Rees, & M. Pieron (Eds.), *Myths, models, and methods in sport pedagogy* (pp. 79-86). Champaign, IL: Human Kinetics.

Siedentop, D. (1990). Games as learning environments in physical education. *Sport Pedagogy* (pp. 111-124). Dankook, Korea: Sport Science Institute.

Siedentop, D. (1991)*: Developing teaching skills in physical education* (3rd ed.). Mountain View, CA: Mayfield.

Siedentop, D., Mand, C., & Taggart, A. (1986). *Physical education: Teaching and curriculum strategies for grades 5-12*. Mountain View, CA: Mayfield.

Sweeney, J., Tannehill, D., & Teeters, L. (1992). Team up for fitness. *Strategies*, **5**(6), 20-23.

United States Olympic Committee Education Committee. (n.d.). *Olympic day in the schools: Focus on excellence*. Champaign, IL: Human Kinetics.

Index

About the Editor

Daryl Siedentop, PED, is a professor in the school of Health, Physical Education and Recreation at The Ohio State University. Dr. Siedentop has worked in curriculum development and the teaching of skill development for two decades, in both classroom and research settings. He is the author of *Physical Education: Introductory Analysis*, the book in which he set forth and developed the "play education" curriculum theory from which his Sport Education Model eventually emerged. He also received the Samaranch Award in 1982 for *Developing Teaching Skills in Physical Education* (2nd ed.). Dr. Siedentop is a Fellow of the American Academy of Kinesiology and Physical Education and a member of the National Association for Sport and Physical Education. He and his wife, Bobbie, live in Columbus, Ohio, where he enjoys golf, reading, and running.